Evangelical Christians are in urgent need of serious, faithful, and intelligent answers to questions every believer confronts. In this series, Owen Strachan and Gavin Peacock honor the gospel and help believers to understand these urgent questions, to think biblically, and to live faithfully.

Albert Mohler
President, The Southern Baptist Theological Seminary,
Louisville, Kentucky

In this series of books Owen Strachan and Gavin Peacock show us how amazingly relevant the Bible is to our smartphone generation. Technology often only conspires with our wandering and warped passions to leave us in a state of enslavement and despair. However, this trilogy points to God's word as our only hope through its holistic teaching on sexuality and through the gospel of God's redeeming grace. I cannot too highly recommend a prayerful study of these books. They might prove a life-saver!

Conrad Mbewe
Pastor of Kabwata Baptist Church, Lusaka, Zambia

We daily awake to a culture saturated with sexual temptation and confused about sexual identity. Instantaneous and worldwide media accelerate and proliferate these sinful ideologies in an unprecedented way. The Bible, however, provides supernatural power to overcome sexual temptation and divine definition for sexual identity. In this straightforward and powerful series, Strachan and Peacock relay a message of hope, transformation, and biblical recalibration because of Christ. These pages are a reveille bugle to wake up a generation sedated by sinful, sexual trajectories. This series is for pastors, parents, and anyone who desires biblical clarity in a world of confusion.

Rick Holland
Pastor, Mission Road Bible Church, Prairie Village, Kansas

Here is an extremely timely trilogy for the cultural crisis in which we find ourselves. Addressing the issue of human sexuality head on, Owen Strachan and Gavin Peacock have delivered a brilliant analysis of the present day crisis over personal sexuality and gender issues. Not only do they make the right diagnosis, they also prescribe the one and only cure for this devastating problem. They offer the transforming power of the saving and sanctifying grace of God. You need to be conversant with the truths in this trilogy.

Steven J. Lawson
President, OnePassion Ministries
Professor, The Master's Seminary, Sun Valley, California
Teaching Fellow, Ligonier Ministries

I enthusiastically endorse this biblical sexuality trilogy on lust, homosexuality and transgenderism, written by men of conviction, who know what God has revealed in His Word and who understand the sinful struggles of fallen humanity. The authors have courageously written about some of the most sensitive issues of our times, denouncing the deviation from God's original design, while always pointing to the person (Christ) who can give us the victory over such sinful desires and behaviors. If there was ever a generation in need of such a trilogy it is ours. What an insightful and powerful tool this will prove to be for the church of our time. These books are biblical, readable, practical and answer many of the questions many are asking. Every pastor, every leader, in fact, every person who wants to be thoroughly informed about these issues should read this trilogy.

Miguel Núñez
President, Ministerios Integridad y Sabiduría
(Dominican Republic)

Strachan and Peacock confront sexual sin where it begins: in the heart. These men understand that Scripture, by the power of God's Spirit, is the only instrument that can confront the sinful lusts that reside in the dark crevices of the heart. With biblical precision and pastoral care, Strachan and Peacock demonstrate the connection between heart desires and sinful behavior. You would do well to heed their biblical warning and instruction to tackle sinful actions by practically confronting sinful desires with the truth of God.

T. Dale Johnson, Jr.
Executive Director, ACBC
Associate Professor of Biblical Counseling,
Midwestern Baptist Theological Seminary, Kansas City,
Missouri

Our twenty-first century world is deeply confused about the meaning of sex. ... This series directly applies biblical truth to urgent matters of human sexuality, and does so with both pastoral sensitivity and theological integrity. All too often the church fails to respond to sexual sin with both compassion and clarity. This series does both, and does so with courage, verve, and an ever-present reminder that Jesus Christ is making all things new.

David Talcott
Assistant Professor, The King's College, New York

This biblically-centered and theologically-robust series on biblical sexuality is a tour de force. There aren't two other theologians I would rather hear from on these vital issues than Strachan and Peacock. Not only do they bring scholarship to bear on the predominant conversation of our culture, but they offer warm pastoral counsel as they seek to redirect this conversation from the public square back to the foundation of Scripture. If you struggle with sexual sin, deal with questions about sexuality in your current ministry context, or desire to learn more about such issues, this trilogy of books is for you.

Dustin W. Benge
Senior fellow, The Andrew Fuller Center for Baptist Studies and professor at Munster Bible College, Cork, Ireland

Today people are wandering in a fog of confusion regarding sexuality. Truth cuts through the fog in this series of books from Owen Strachan and Gavin Peacock. They have laid out the simple order of biblical teaching on the most contested debates about sexuality. Testimonies and frequently-asked-questions illustrate the practical usefulness of the bible's teaching. I have witnessed the compassion, wisdom and usefulness of this teaching being applied in Gavin's ministry at our church. The result is that these books are floodlights in the worldly storm. They don't claim to be exhaustive, but neither are they exhausting. They offer much-needed confidence to regular Christians on pilgrimage in this new dark age. But most of all, this trilogy highlights the compassion of Jesus Christ in the gospel. Read these books, share them with others, and let hope pierce the present darkness.

Clint Humfrey
Senior Pastor, Calvary Grace Church, Calgary, Alberta

This is a timely trilogy, and a manly one that ladies will also love. Name three topics hotter than these today in society, and any areas where the Christian home and Church more urgently needs equipping than in matters of gender and sexuality? I've already begun walking through this series with my sons, and it has sparked great discussions. Pastor Peacock and Scholar Strachan form a rare combination and a dynamic duo in this thoroughly biblical response to the 'strong winds of culture' that are blowing. They offer not just a 'battle cry', but also a 'declaration of hope'. With a high view of Scripture and of the local church, and a right view of humanity, they bring gospel remedies and clear answers to the most thorny questions. The FAQs alone are worth the price of each book!

Tim Cantrell
Senior Pastor, Antioch Bible Church & President of Shepherds' Seminary in Johannesburg, South Africa

In a world where sex has become everything, anything, and nothing, Strachan and Peacock do a masterful job at helping the church recover and keep a Biblical theology of sexuality. Their series reminds us that God is the author of life and He has not released His copyright on the creation. Sex is His gift, gender

His distinction, marriage His idea, and true love His nature. Any definition of sexual identity or pursuit of sexual intimacy cannot be rightly achieved apart from obedience to God. As the authors argue, the path to true sexual fulfillment is one decided by the gospel, not our glands. In a sex-crazed world, here are wise words that are timely, truthful, and transformative!

Philip De Courcy
Pastor of Kindred Community Church in Anaheim Hills, California;
Bible teacher on the daily radio program 'Know the Truth'

The terrible times of the last days are dominated by 'feel good' culture which has misled millions onto the destructive super-highway of illicit sex in its different forms. From Scripture, research and the experiences of individuals Peacock and Strachan expose the lies that tried and tested societal norms are bad and 'follow your heart' is good. This series is humble and hard-hitting – saying what needs to be said but which many Christian leaders have been afraid to say. However, this is no mere condemnatory diatribe pointing the finger. These pages are full of compassion. There is practical help for those struggling and a triumphant note that though sexual sin is overwhelming the power of the Lord Jesus Christ is greater. This is a very valuable piece of work.

John Benton
Director for Pastoral Support at the Pastors' Academy, London Seminary, London

Owen Strachan and Gavin Peacock are men full of biblical wisdom and conviction. And that's precisely what the church needs in this hour. The authors bring their wisdom and conviction to bear in this work as they engage some of the most pressing issues confronting the church. I heartily recommend this work to every gospel minister—and the church members they serve.

Jason K. Allen
President, Midwestern Baptist Theological Seminary & Spurgeon College, Kansas City, Missouri

The gospel of Jesus is good news not only because it secures eternal life for the believer, but also because it transforms this life, here and now. This is no less true with respect to the contested intersection of gender, sex, and identity. In this trilogy, Strachan and Peacock show how the gospel renews fallen sexuality and brings wholeness according to God's good design. Anyone curious about what the Bible teaches on sexuality and what biblical obedience looks like will want to use these pithy volumes to grow and disciple others into faithful maturity.

Colin J. Smothers
Executive Director, Council on Biblical Manhood and Womanhood

WHAT DOES THE BIBLE
TEACH ABOUT
HOMOSEXUALITY?

OWEN STRACHAN & GAVIN PEACOCK

CHRISTIAN
FOCUS

Scripture quotations are from *The Holy Bible, English Standard Version*, copyright © 2001 by Crossway Bibles, a publishing ministry of Good News Publishers. Used by permission. All rights reserved. ESV Text Edition: 2011.

hardback ISBN 978-1-5271-0477-8
epub ISBN 978-1-5271-0579-9
mobi ISBN 978-1-5271-0580-5

10 9 8 7 6 5 4 3 2 1

First published in 2020
by
Christian Focus Publications Ltd,
Geanies House, Fearn, Ross-shire,
IV20 1TW, Great Britain

www.christianfocus.com

Cover by Peter Matthess

Printed and bound
by Gutenberg Press Ltd, Malta

CONTENTS

Introduction.. 15

1. The Bible on Homosexuality..........................29

2. The Transforming Power of the Gospel 69

3. The Faithful Fight Against Sexual Sin........ 107

Frequently Asked Questions 131

Acknowledgements... 147

About the Center for Biblical Sexuality 149

Dedication

To Dan Michaud and Tony Roake

*Pastors who gave us a model
of truth, kindness, and
perseverance*

All Scripture is breathed out by God and profitable for teaching, for reproof, for correction, and for training in righteousness, that the man of God may be complete, equipped for every good work.

(2 Tim. 3:16-17)

INTRODUCTION

━━━━━━

There are few actors around who have the range and presence of Tom Hardy. He was terrifying as Bane; cunning in extremity in *The Revenant*; and noble beyond words, gallantly sacrificing his own safety to shoot down enemy fighters, in *Dunkirk*.[1] One of Hardy's most noteworthy performances came, however, not in film but in an interview. Hardy is known for being less than irrepressible on occasion in public events, and when a reporter asked him—repeatedly—whether he was homosexual, Hardy barely answered. Here's the awkward play-by-play as it occurred in 2015:

> **GC:** *Given interviews you've done in the past, your own sexuality seems a bit more ambiguous. Do you find it hard for celebrities to talk to media about their sexuality?*
>
> **TH:** *What on earth are you on about?*

---

1   We're not going to talk about *Venom*.

GC: I was referring to an interview given to *Attitude* magazine a few years ago.

TH: But what is your question?

GC: I was wondering if you find it difficult for celebrities to talk about their sexuality?

TH: I don't find it difficult for celebrities to talk about their sexuality. Are you asking about my sexuality?

GC: Um … sure.

TH: Why?

TH: Thank you (awkward laughter, end of conversation).

This strange little moment made just a blip in the media when it happened.[2] But it stuck in my mind. It seems to sum up much of how our culture encourages us to think today. We have little privacy (and celebrities seem to have none). We feel no hesitation about making conversations sexual in public. Perhaps most significantly, we are in an age that seems to define itself by sexuality. To put this differently, we are encouraged to think of ourselves *as* our sexuality. I am my sexual preferences.

---

2   See 'Tom Hardy responds to sexuality question: "What are you on about?" – video,' *The Guardian*, September 15, 2015, accessible at https://www.theguardian.com/film/video/2015/sep/15/tom-hardy-sexuality-question-legend-video. Last accessed January 2020.

This is a very, very important matter before us. In our time, sexuality—always important for humanity—has become the defining issue and identity-marker of our time. Ours is a sexual age. But this is true in a different way than, say, the 'free love' era of the 1960s. Then, sexuality was more associated with behavior. The sexual revolution encouraged people to 'do whatever they wanted' with sexual partners. Today, the late stages of the sexual revolution encourage us in a slightly different way to 'be whomever we want.' Our sexuality is a very important part of this being. The focus has shifted, you could say, from behavior to identity. Sex isn't just something I do (however I see fit). Sex is something I am. It's me. Again: I am my sexuality.[3]

There is much for Christians to think through, carefully and compassionately, on this matter.

---

3 Some key terms related to LGBT identity from the Human Rights Campaign. 'Gay: A person who is emotionally, romantically or sexually attracted to members of the same sex. Lesbian: A woman who is emotionally, romantically or sexually attracted to other women. LGBTQ: An acronym for "lesbian, gay, bisexual, transgender and queer." Sexual orientation: An inherent or immutable enduring emotional, romantic or sexual attraction to other people.' See 'Glossary of Terms,' Human Rights Coalition, accessible at https://www.hrc.org/resources/glossary-of-terms. Last accessed January 2020. Note the FAQ at book's end, where we engage some such terms.

We must give a good answer, a biblical and Christ-shaped answer, to the major questions of our time. People all around us are finding their identity in their sexuality, including homosexuality. Many today are confused and even trapped by the culture's teaching; they don't know what to make of it, and they struggle to know whether it is true or not. There is a range of experience regarding homosexuality: some people advocate it as the cause of our time, some celebrate it in a personal way, some are confused by their desires, some have homosexual inclinations but do not want them. There is sadly little nuance in our cultural conversation over homosexuality, and little help for those who want good biblical answers to these momentous questions.[4]

Thankfully, the Bible gives us the clarity and help we all need, whatever our background,

---

4   Diverse voices that have driven this conversation in the last half-century or more include Lesléa Newman, *Heather Has Two Mommies* (New York: Alyson, 1989); Gore Vidal, *Myra Breckenridge* (New York: Little, Brown, 1968); Alfred Kinsey, *Sexual Behavior in the Human Male* (1948) and *Sexual Behavior in the Human Female* (1953), to cite just a few. To better understand the development of the sexual revolution, see R. Albert Mohler, Jr., *We Must Not Be Silent: Speaking Truth to a Culture Redefining Sex, Marriage, and the Very Meaning of Right and Wrong* (Nashville: Thomas Nelson, 2016), pp. 28ff.

whatever our temptation patterns. Our sexuality is a key part of us, as we will show in this little book. Sexuality isn't something human beings made up. Sexuality is a gift and stewardship from God. But even as we make plain in these pages that sexuality is God-given, we will also make clear that there is much more to human identity than sexuality. Here's a small sampling of what forms our identity. We are image-bearers. We are spiritual by nature, made to know God. We are men or women. Humanity is not an accident. We are not a mere collection of cells; we are not atoms colliding. We are not self-conscious consciousness. We are people, and God made us by His own breath and by His own hand.

What Is My Identity, Exactly?

So, let's think once more about the original question: am I my sexuality? Well, sexuality is a core part of who we are. But no, you and I are not our sexuality. By this we mean that our sexual preference, our pattern of sexual attraction, is not the most important truth about us. God wants our sexuality to glorify Him, to be sure. Manhood and womanhood are vitally important, further, to knowing who we are – these are foundational realities in every sense. But this is a quite different personal marker than finding our identity in our sexual urges. Along these lines, you do not become a fully-functioning human being when you can most clearly pinpoint your deepest sexual instincts. In similar terms, you do not discover your true self when you start being sexually active with your preferred partner. Finally, you will not find lasting happiness when you embrace your attraction patterns, whether homosexual, heterosexual, or otherwise.

The reason for all this is that we cannot find true hope and lasting fulfillment in ourselves. Our sinful hearts are naturally bent this way, but this project of self-actualization—really, self-salvation—will not and cannot work. Though we all try to save ourselves in some way, we cannot make ourselves right. Something has gone terribly wrong in us, and there is no personal discovery, no sexual awakening, that will make us whole. We cannot be our own functional savior, and neither can any person, any system of thought, or any lifestyle.

Are Christians Anti-Gay?

We start here because many people are being told a lie about their sexuality. There are various behaviors and lifestyles that have gained approval in Western culture in recent years, but few that have become more a celebrated identity than that of homosexual, by which we mean a person who identifies as being drawn sexually to the same sex. We are told by a secular culture that homosexuality is good and acceptable, no different than being 'heterosexual.' More commonly, those who disagree with positive presentations of homosexuality draw condemnation, censure, and policing. In a 'tolerant' age that supposedly seeks equality and fairness for all, failure to approve of homosexuality means very intolerant responses indeed.

We need to be clear that our culture misunderstands the church of Christ on this point. Speaking against the sin of homosexuality is taken today as denying the humanity of people who have—and in some cases have always had—patterns of same-sex attraction (SSA). If we call people out of homosexuality, then, we are effectively dehumanizing them, for their sexuality is their identity. We are doing violence, in other words, to their person. But this is not what believers mean in this conversation. We who have been called out of darkness call sinners of every kind out of darkness, including sexual lostness of every form (and there are many).

It is surely possible for Christians to err in this conversation. We all are a work in progress when it comes to communication of the truth; we all must pray for much grace to 'speak the truth in love'

(Eph. 4:15). When the truth is challenged, we can fail in different ways: we can under-speak, and say too little, thus robbing God of the glory He reaps from courageous witness, or we can over-speak, possibly communicating that homosexual people are not real human people given their wickedness.

We see here that believers *could* be 'anti-gay' in a sinful way, hating certain individuals. This sadly happens. Wherever we see such behavior, true believers decry it. But the Bible itself, and Christians who proclaim biblical truth, are not 'anti-gay.' We in fact love fellow sinners of every kind, and we love them enough to tell them the truth about their lostness and need for Jesus. They may not welcome this witness; they may not see it as loving; they may accuse us of all sorts of evildoing. But while we strive to reason with all people, we know that we cannot manage other peoples' view of us. We can only seek to love God, proclaim God's truth, and live according to it by the Spirit's indwelling power.

The Bible Speaks Clearly About Homosexuality

With all due caveats noted, we must be clear: the Bible, as we shall see, does not offer a single word of praise for homosexuality. It is quite the opposite. From start to finish, the Bible speaks with one voice against homosexuality, presenting it as unrighteous, ungodly, and tangible rebellion in bodily form against God. These words sound very strong today, we know. They do not mesh with the spirit of the age. But hard as they may be to receive, they reflect the teaching of Scripture.

Scripture is sometimes presented as a book of myths and fairy tales. Others see it as a collection of life principles, a religious encyclopedia for moral living. Still others regard it as a handbook to prosperity and wealth. But the Bible is quite different than it is said to be. The Bible is the very mind and will of God. The Bible is God-breathed, such that every word is inspired by the Holy Spirit; accordingly, the Bible is inerrant, without error in all it teaches; thus the Bible is authoritative, the standard of all standards; so the Bible is fully sufficient, fitted perfectly to purify us and conform us to God's holy standard. The Bible is not one religious book among many, therefore; the Bible is the very Word of God, the truth we need to form a worldview, understand our lives, and live for God's glory.[5]

---

5   To understand this brief theology of Scripture, see texts like Numbers 23:19; Psalm 119; John 1, 8, and 16; 2 Timothy 3:16; 2 Peter 1:3-11, 21. For a readable resource on this doctrine, see J. I. Packer, *Truth & Power: The Place of Scripture in the Christian Life* (Wheaton, Illinois: Harold Shaw, 1996).

In its unfolding narrative, a grand story that is true and good and beautiful, we learn who God is, who we are, what has gone wrong in the world, and how all things will be made right. The Bible gives us reality, in other words. It indicts sinners of every conceivable kind (and there are many). Though some argue that the Bible targets only one sin or one group of sinners, it does not. Quite the opposite: the Bible shows that every single person has fallen short of God's glory and deserves eternal personal punishment from God in hell for their sin.[6]

God's Word opens our eyes to see truth we did not know before, or did not *want* to know before. The Bible thus seeks to accomplish the reverse of what we often want it to do for us. We come to God's Word expecting it to *affirm* us. But the Scripture instead seeks to awaken us. What

---

See also the two helpful statements of the International Council on Biblical Inerrancy, one on inerrancy, the other on hermeneutics: http://www.alliancenet.org/the-chicago-statement-on-biblical-inerrancy and http://www.alliancenet.org/the-chicago-statement-on-biblical-hermeneutics. Last accessed January 2020.

6 In this book, as in this trilogy, we're writing about what the Bible teaches. In doing so, we do not discount other legitimate fields, and we recognize that sin yields complexity, and complexity requires careful spiritual help. But the Bible is our 'norming authority'; in other words, it shapes all our thinking and doing.

is the distinction here? Simply this: though the sinful human heart craves approval of our natural lifestyle, the Word of God instead shows us that we need something much, much greater than mere approval. We need heart change. We need soul salvation. We need total transformation. This is true of every last one of us – no exceptions.

What Will We Seek: Affirmation or Salvation?

God gives us what need, we now understand: He comes to us, dead in our sin, and He makes us alive. He who created the human race by His Word finds us and re-creates us by the Word (John 1:1-18). This re-creation is anything but partial, halfway, or inadequate. Salvation in the name of Christ does not equate to joining a Facebook group. Redemption does not mean getting a new necklace with a little cross displayed on it. Transformation does not look like putting a bumper sticker on your car. As Steve Lawson has said, when God saves a sinner, He does not execute a makeover. He executes a takeover. This is divine rescue, divine re-creation, divine remaking.

This little book represents our attempt to trumpet this good news. We are a partnership, if you will; Owen is a theologian with pastoral concern, and Gavin is a pastor with theological concern.[7] We both believe that there is something greater in this world than man's fame, man's praise, and man's affirmation. Every human heart desires these things, as we will see in Chapter 1; even after trusting Christ, we still must constantly fight such instincts, repent of sins of the mind, heart, will, and body, and return to the truths of God. How glorious that we can do so; how glorious that God lives to save and transform sinners like us, as we will see in Chapter 2. As we will see, coming to Christ does not magically wipe away all our challenges and struggles; in Chapter 3 we'll give practical advice—grounded in truth—to defeat sin and exalt Jesus. We'll close things with a special section giving some short answers to frequently asked questions (FAQ) based on the content.

As is apparent, this book is grounded in the total inspiration, inerrancy, authority, sufficiency, and clarity of the Bible. We're not psychologists, sociologists, doctors, life coaches, or activists. We're teachers of the Word. That's what we provide in these pages in generally simple

---

7   Owen has invested much time and energy in researching and writing on these matters, producing scholarship of various kinds on these theological subjects. Gavin has counseled widely in his church, working with people of various sexual sin patterns (and many others besides), and has seen many people affected and changed by God's grace as a result of the application of sound doctrine.

sentences, without a ton of footnotes or academic discussion. Our hope is that ordinary men and women just like us find real guidance and real help through our pointing to the Scripture and its teaching on a difficult reality. Biblical compassion and care, we see, is not divorced from the truth; instead, it is dependent on it.

Conclusion

God made sexuality. This is a crucial part of who we are: men and women for His glory. But we are not sexual beings in cultural terms. We were not made for this world alone. We were not made for small things and earthly causes. We were made for eternity, where the church will be married to Christ. Let us venture forward, then, and look at the very sobering words of God about homosexuality. We need to receive the sure warning of the Lord about man's depravity. There are many ways to die; there are many ways to go to hell. This is one of them, and one that our culture celebrates today. Let us flee that trap, escaping if necessary with the fire of heaven singeing our clothes. We do not run into the wilderness, though. We run straight into the arms of Christ, the Savior who welcomes repentant sinners of every kind to a kingdom not built with man's strength, but with the very power and grace of God.

1. THE BIBLE ON HOMOSEXUALITY

As we saw in the Introduction, one of the areas that most draws our attention, that most consumes us, is our sexuality. This has always been a reality for humanity; but in 2020, we are encouraged in a special way to focus on our sexual identity and 'orientation.'[1] We hear many things today about our sexuality. On the one hand, we hear that it is fixed and unmovable. Think of the 'I can't change' narrative of recent years; one hit song by the rapper Macklemore became a global anthem for articulating just this line. No doubt many people continue to think this is true. Their sexuality is who they are, foundational to their existence, shaping every part of their being.

How interesting, then, that our contemporary culture also says exactly the opposite as well. Different voices—many of them also associated with the

---

1 An 'orientation' as is commonly understood refers to our pattern of attraction.

'LGBT' movement—tell us that our identity is not at all fixed. Instead, it is fluid. It's not nailed down; it's ever-evolving. The 'genderqueer' category seeks to capture this experience, as does the '+' in some LGBT formulations. There is no male and female 'binary,' and as such, there is not even a defined sexual pattern, whether heterosexual (attracted to the opposite sex) or homosexual (attracted to the same sex). Such thinking is old-school and outmoded. My sexuality, friends tell us today, is beyond categorization. It transcends existing paradigms. It is not tied-down; it is shifting, moving, dynamic.[2]

Wherever people land on the changeableness of our identity, we cannot miss that our culture seeks to persuade that our identity fundamentally is sexual. We remember, for example, what Michel Foucault once said: sex is 'more important than our soul.'[3] But what does the Bible teach us about our sexuality? In a previous book, we looked closely at the issue of lust; specifically, we focused on the issue of opposite-sex lust. In this book, we want to look at the area of homosexuality. What does the Bible teach about it? How is the Bible's

---

2   Ironically, the embrace of 'non-binary' identity merely creates a new binary: non-binary and binary.

3   Michel Foucault, *The History of Sexuality*, vol. 1, *An Introduction*, trans. Robert Hurley (1978; New York: Vintage Books, 1990), pp. 78, 156.

teaching supposed to impact our thinking? How does knowing Jesus Christ as Savior and Lord affect same-sex identity, thinking, attraction, and behavior? In the pages that follow in this chapter, we will walk through the Bible's presentation of same-sex attraction and homosexuality. We will see that the Scripture has a fundamentally different word on these matters than our modern culture.

The Good Design of God: We Are God's Image

The Bible's first words that help us understand homosexuality do not speak explicitly of it. Instead, in Genesis 1 we learn two major truths: firstly that every human person is made in God's image, and secondly that God has made all people either a man or a woman. We have traced these ideas in *The Grand Design* (and in book one of this trilogy), but we must consider them briefly once more. Genesis 1:26-8 tells us crucial material about our identity as human people:

> Then God said, 'Let us make man in our image, after our likeness. And let them have dominion over the fish of the sea and over the birds of the heavens and over the livestock and over all the earth and over every creeping thing that creeps on the earth.'

So God created man in his own image,
*   in the image of God he created him;*
*   male and female he created them.*

And God blessed them. And God said to them, 'Be fruitful and multiply and fill the earth and subdue it, and have dominion over the fish of the sea and over the birds of the heavens and over every living thing that moves on the earth.'

The first truth about humanity is not that we are sexual beings. By this I mean we are not taught here to construe our identity in terms of our sexual preference. Instead, we are taught that the human race is the race that images the glory of God. In a very distant way, we look like God, and point to God as our Creator. The image of God isn't a quality one has—like eye color or intelligence or skin tone or relational status—but rather is who we are. We are the image of God (see 1 Cor. 11:7 on this point).[4] We can't change this or alter it. It's true of us, of every single human person, no matter what.

We need to see that this is a very different starting point than secular starting points. The human person has a fixed identity in the biblical

---

4   See Owen Strachan, *Reenchanting Humanity: A Theology of Mankind* (Fearn: Ross-Shire, Christian Focus, 2019), pp. 7-50.

mind. We're not a mere collection of cells. We're not a cosmic accident. We haven't randomly evolved into the human form we possess. No, God made us specially for His glory. We exist because He wanted us to exist. We have shape and form because He wanted us to have shape and form. We have dignity and purpose and worth—every single human being does—because God is our Maker. This is true before the fall, and it is also true after the fall. We are fully human as God-made beings. Nothing can change that.

The strikingly spiritual nature of humanity stands out in Genesis 1:26-8. Our culture tells us that we are a sexual being above all, but Scripture tells us that we are a spiritual being above all. This is true of everyone. The human race was made to know God. We were not made for ourselves. We were not made for sin. We were made by God for God. We do not gain or exude value when we become sexually desirable or sexually active. Our culture teaches us this, but not the Bible. In the teaching of Genesis 1, we have value and worth and dignity because God made us. He made us so that we would live for His glory and fulfill His purposes in the earth.

This is the very opposite of what we so often hear today. We are enmeshed in cultures that tell us that our sexuality is who we are. This is especially true of our non-Christian contexts, in which it is basically assumed that we will engage in sexual activity at the earliest possible opportunity. Men and women who instead choose chastity before marriage, and gladly remain virgins, seem shockingly weird. But such a choice is in no way weird. We may be called to marriage or not, but sex is not what makes us human. God forming us in His image is what makes us human. Our 'imageness' is the first truth about us. We are in our being the likeness of God. He is our Maker; we are His image.

In learning this first truth about our humanity, we gain an absolutely vital truth about our identity. In the Bible, you don't make up your identity from scratch. In the Bible, our personal identity is created by God. True, there are elements about ourselves that we learn over time – that's a great part of life. Yet in biblical terms, human identity is not a great project by which we choose, from scratch, who we wish to be. In God's design, we have a certain body, a certain family background, eye color, hair color, genetic predispositions, and much more from our debut on the earth. Our identity is not self-created, but is God-given.

The Good Design of God: We Are Men or Women for His Glory

We learn a second glorious truth in this section of Genesis 1: that God made men and women. Right after the first truth of humanity, our image-bearing nature, we learn that manhood and womanhood owe their origin to Almighty God. God made us this way in order to fulfill the purposes He set before us, to take 'dominion' of the earth, a mission that includes numerous duties, including the population of this globe by marital procreation (v. 28). Only a man and a woman can 'multiply,' after all. We see in the very first chapter of the Bible that God's design is not static, but active, and that God has a certain design for men and women that leads into glorification of His name. God loves life, clearly. Only the sexual union of a man and a woman can produce it.

This design ceases to be principal in Genesis 2. In this chapter, it becomes a reality. In Genesis 2, we learn that God specially made the man and the woman (vv. 7, 22). The Lord formed the sexes by His own agency. He is the one who created manhood in physical form, and He is the one who created womanhood in physical form. He designed marriage for one man and one woman. Adam and Eve are brought together by the Creator in a garden wedding ceremony; they are 'naked and not ashamed' (Gen. 2:25).

This tells us what the holy design of God was for all humanity. Whatever each person's precise calling in life, human sexuality has just one righteous expression: marital love. Sexuality, therefore, is not a force within us that we may express however we see fit. Sexual desire has only one appropriate end and outlet: the covenant of marriage. Sexual intimacy honors God only when one man and one woman join together in wedded love. God has not given humanity sexual capacity for any and every desired activity; God has given humanity sexual capacity to drive us into marriage according to His call.

Let's spell this out a little further. There are numerous nuances we need to cover briefly in order to avoid confusion on this count. This material will be important later in the book as we discuss what conversion entails for our sexuality; before we get to the transformation created by the gospel, though, we need to trace the five-fold blueprint of biblical sexuality created by the Lord (introduced in Book One of this trilogy). First, we can identify *complementary unity*. Here we mean what we introduced above: that the man and the woman are made in God's image (Gen. 1:26-8). The man is formed first, and the woman is formed from his body. This order of creation matters, and matters greatly in the life of the church (see 1 Tim. 2:9-15).[5] Even as the order of creation establishes the man's leadership in the home and the church, the sexes alike bear God's image and give Him glory. There are no grounds, then, for any unequal view of men and women; men and women alike possess God-given dignity and worth as those made in the image of God. Men and women are unified in creation, made for a shared mission of dominion in all the earth.

Secondly, we can identify *complementary polarity* in biblical sexuality. Here we mean that the sexes—though fully unified—are made distinct by God. The man and the woman share humanity, but do not share manhood and womanhood. They have different bodies, different bodily workings, and different roles and duties that flow from God-given distinctiveness (Gen. 1:27; 2–3). Of course, there is a spectrum of difference between men and women; we overlap in many respects in both creation (God's original design) and new creation (who we become in Christ). Yet we are right to see throughout Scripture (and throughout our own

---

5   We note at this point that the roles of men and women flow out of the design of God and the order of creation (1 Tim. 2:9-15). From our God-given sex, then, flows our God-given role in life.

experience in this world) that the sexes are distinct in many ways, and that this distinctiveness is to the glory of God.

From our earliest days, we are a man or a woman, a boy or a girl, and our body tells us which we are. Yet we are not made to be apart; the sexes are made for one another. We call this third theological concept *complementary reciprocity*. Whether a man is married or not, he is a man made by God who is called to embrace biblical manhood. In ideal terms, his father trains him to be a leader, protector, and provider for the good of himself and others. Whether a woman is married or not, she is a woman made by God who is called to embrace biblical womanhood. In ideal terms, her mother shows her how to be a nurturer of children, worker in the home, and supporter of godly men.

In the biblical mind, a man or woman may or may not have any desire for marriage, but they nonetheless see themselves as a godly man or woman. They recognize the goodness and blessedness of the opposite sex (Gen. 2; 1 Tim. 5). They see that God made the sexes to work together in complementary fashion. Men and women are made to face one another, regardless of marital call. We are not generically Christian before, during, or after marriage. We always relate to one another as a Christian man or Christian woman.

We are always living life either as a Christian man or a Christian woman. We are always striving to embrace the fullness of biblical manhood or biblical womanhood. We are always trying to encourage brothers and sisters in the faith to do the same.

Trusting Christ entails all this. Though most people are called to marriage, conversion in Jesus' name does not mean 'becoming straight' or 'having sexual attraction for the opposite sex' or 'getting married.' It does mean that we embrace what Paul calls 'nature' and 'natural' functioning, thinking, and living in the power of Christ (see Rom. 1:26-7). As we shall discuss in Chapters 2 and 3, where we have strayed from being a biblical man, we embrace biblical manhood. Where we have strayed from being a biblical woman, we embrace biblical womanhood. This is what holiness looks like, in fact: it looks like wrapping our arms fully around our call to honor God as a man or a woman. There are numerous practical effects to work out here; for now, it is enough to sketch these things and fill them out more later.[6]

---

6   To learn more about biblical manhood and womanhood, we commend John Piper and Wayne Grudem, eds., *Recovering Biblical Manhood & Womanhood: A Response to Evangelical Feminism* (Wheaton: Crossway, 2006 [1991]).

How Should We Think About Opposite-Sex Interest?

There are two additional dimensions to God's creational, complementary design. God has given many what we may call, fourthly, *complementary interest*. As covered in Book One of this trilogy, by this phrase we mean that as many boys and girls come of age, they will find an interest in the opposite sex developing in them. These stirrings, as we have articulated already, are a key part of how the human race continues to 'multiply' and 'fill the earth' to God's glory. Of course, we are not speaking of any lustful desire here. As we have discussed in Book One, Scripture does not endorse sinful lust. So we must distinguish here between a 'natural' and innocent interest in the opposite sex on the one hand, and lustful sexual interest on the other.

Some men and women will not have such interest, whether in their youth or full adulthood. There are various factors at play here. Some will not initially have interest in the opposite sex, but then will find such an instinct developing in them as they mature in their understanding of Scripture and God's design. We need to handle this matter carefully, for there is not in every case a one-size-fits-all experience for our romantic interest in the opposite sex. It can ebb and flow; it can depend on our home environment; it can change over time; or we may never sense it developing in us. The Bible does not teach us that having complementary interest in the opposite sex is the nature or essence of godliness, nor does it teach us that trusting Christ automatically unleashes such feelings. Some may have this experience, and some may not.

Nonetheless, we need to point out that complementary interest accords with God's creational design and plan for men and women to marry, 'multiply,' and fill the earth. Such interest is not a neutral reality; it is a part of how humanity fulfills God's mandate to have dominion over all the earth. We are not faced with a choice in biblical terms, then, between supporting complementary interest or supporting lifelong singleness. We may affirm each calling, and make room for both in the life of the local church, always recognizing that marriage is the calling for most.

This leads into the fifth dimension of a proper understanding of God's design: a *complementary desire for marriage*. As we have noted, it is right and holy to desire marriage. The desire to be married, including the hope of one-flesh union in a righteous way, is good. We should teach this plainly to our children and our churches. When a man prays for marriage to one woman, or a woman asks the Lord to bless her with a godly husband, we must be very clear that Genesis 2, Song of Songs, Matthew 19, and Ephesians 5 (among other texts) show us that these prayers of righteous saints honor the Lord and His beautiful design. As we traced in Book One, it is good to honor marriage, and it is good to want it. No shame attaches to this longing; no condemnation comes from wanting to join with a godly member of the opposite sex in lifelong covenantal union.

In talking about the complementary desire for marriage, we clearly do not mean marriage to anyone. Here we must be very clear: biblical marriage is not whatever you make it. Biblical marriage *is* a man and a woman joined together for life. Scripture begins with the marriage of Adam and Eve in Eden, celebrates marriage throughout its narrative, and climaxes with the marriage of Christ and His blood-bought church in the New Jerusalem (see Gen. 2; Song; Rev. 21).[7]

---

7   On this point, see Raymond Ortlund, Jr., *Marriage and the Mystery of the Gospel*, Short Studies in Biblical Theology (Wheaton, Illinois: Crossway, 2016). Regeneration is more than merely being 'restored' to God's creation design; we are made men and women of the new covenant in Christ, and have already begun to be what we will be in eternity. While affirming our full participation in Edenic design, we do not find our ultimate fulfillment in it, but

Marriage in earthly and spiritual terms is always complementary, consisting of a manly head and a submissive bride (see Eph. 5:22-33). All this means that if we think marriage is simply covenantal companionship with anyone we desire (perhaps of the same sex, for example), we miss the biblical mark.

The preceding discussion reminds us: the design of God for sex is good and beautiful and joyful. Adam rejoiced when the Lord gave him a wife. He sings a song, it seems, of praise to God as he names the woman God has made (Gen. 2:23). Adam's aloneness was not good; it was in fact the only non-good detail of the created world. But once God makes the woman from his rib, Adam is no longer alone. He has been given the gift of marriage, a state that depends upon manhood and womanhood. In Scripture, marriage depends upon the complementary sexes, upon manhood and womanhood. Marriage is designed to display the beauty of complementarity, of the man and woman who are each image-bearers but are distinct from one another. They complement one another in every way, with their bodies signaling the distinctive beauty of God's design.[8]

---

in the Christ-church marriage of the new covenant that builds off of Eden and brings it to completion.

8 In general terms, Dutch theologian Herman Bavinck sketches the distinctive traits of the sexes, connecting

But though this is a lovely design, things go awry. The woman follows the serpent instead of the Sovereign. The man does not keep God's charge to 'watch over' the garden (Gen. 2:15). He stands passively by as Satan attacks his wife and leads her to sin against God by eating the fruit of the tree of the knowledge of good and evil. Adam and Eve are then plunged into sin and banished from Eden. Satan's assault on the good plan of God is successful, and the world falls under the shadow of the curse.

In a post-Genesis 3 world, every human person has a sinful nature. We were not made this way; we were not formed to be sinners. We were made by God, and created to know Him and love Him. But now we hate Him. Now we are far from Him. Now we rebel against Him in too many ways to count.[9] Instead of fundamentally following His will and way, we walk our own path. Our hearts chase

---

that distinctiveness to God's good design: 'It is the beauty of loftiness that the man embodies, even as the beauty of comeliness is the possession of the woman.... He engenders respect, she engenders tenderness.' Bavinck, *The Christian Family*, trans. Nelson D. Kloosterman (Grand Rapids: Christian's Library Press, 2012), p. 69.

9   This means, as stated earlier, that humanity is not vaguely 'broken'; we are legally guilty and totally depraved. See John Murray, *The Imputation of Adam's Sin* (Phillipsburg, NJ: P&R, 1977 [1959]), p. 91.

after many things, and we all naturally believe the lie that we can find happiness without God.

The Frightening Witness of Sodom and Gomorrah

God's good plan was never for humanity to fall away from Him. He set Eden up in a way that would give Him maximum glory and bring maximum blessing to His creation. But because Adam and Eve sinned against Him, God acted. He did not only act once against human sinfulness, though. When the wickedness of the world increased, He essentially de-created the world in the days of Noah, sending a terrible flood that overwhelmed the earth. Following this, He essentially re-created the world, promising never to send another flood. But then the wickedness of human people increased once more. We see this in the story of Lot, a resident of Sodom. The Lord's dealings with this city show us that God is not asleep regarding evil. He is the judge of all the earth.[10]

---

10 It is also true that the Lord shows Himself to be the covenant-keeping God in this sordid story. He swore not to destroy the earth again after the great flood, promising this to Noah; so He does not destroy the whole earth for Sodom's sin, but rather isolates His judgment. On the nature of the biblical covenants, see Thomas R. Schreiner, *Covenant and God's Purpose for the World* (Wheaton, Illinois: Crossway, 2018), pp. 19-29.

The story told in Genesis 19 is strange and fascinating. Angels come to Lot, and initially say they will sleep in the 'town square' (v. 2). Lot insists, however, that they rest in his home for the night, and so they do (Gen. 19:3). So far, so hospitable. But then things take a vicious turn. '[A]ll the people to the last man' of Sodom surround Lot's house and demand that he send out his guests. Why? They make it plain: 'that we may know them' (v. 5). Lot knows just what they mean. He goes out, bars the door, and calls them to their face to 'not act so wickedly' (v. 7). Then he says something truly shocking, offering the mob his 'two daughters' to 'do to them as you please' (v. 8). In the span of a few words, we go from great thankfulness at Lot's courage to stupefied horror at Lot's proposal. Rarely has a 'solution' been worse than this one.[11]

The mob ignores this hideous suggestion. They surge ahead to enter the home and seize the angels. But the angels overpower them. They draw Lot back indoors and then afflict the crowd 'with blindness' that disarms them (v. 11). The angels then tell Lot to gather his family for destruction of Sodom is at hand. Indeed, 'the Lord has sent us to destroy it' (v. 13). Lot warns his future sons-in-

---

11 It is of course true that the crowd is being inhospitable here, but this is only the merest glimpse of the problem.

law of the impending sentence, but they think he is joking around (v. 14). Here we see that not taking sin seriously is no new problem. It is an ancient one. Then as now, people laugh as the earth trembles. They do not know that the dam of God's justice, His perfect moral rule, is about to burst. They think they are playing a game, when they are dancing on the precipice of eternity, seconds from death.

Lot and his family leave Sodom. They do not do so with the urgency the situation requires, but they leave nonetheless, albeit with considerable assistance from the angels (vv. 15-22). This is not a time for half-measures; there is no other course of action. 'Escape for your life,' the angels tell him. 'Do not look back or stop anywhere in the valley. Escape to the hills, lest you be swept away' (v. 17). When the fury of God bears down on a people, there is only one option: escape. A headlong dash for the hills. Not stopping, not looking back, not lingering.

Then it comes. The wrath of God rains down on Sodom and Gomorrah. 'Sulfur and fire' pour down from the heavens (v. 24). These cities are ruined, smoldering and burning. Even Lot's family is affected, for his wife looks back—disobeying God's direction—and is turned into a pillar of salt (v. 26). The scene is a real historical event, but it is also an early biblical picture of what happens to the unrepentant. God is not far off. God is not taken aback by sin. God hates sin of any kind, and He hated the sin of Sodom and Gomorrah. He reacted to it with vengeance of a most terrible kind: 'behold, the smoke of the land went up like the smoke of a furnace' (v. 28).

This is not just any scene. The Lord was vexed by the sin of Sodom and Gomorrah in a unique way. The New Testament makes clear that God hated this sin. He made 'them an example of what is going to happen to the ungodly,' according to 2 Peter 2:6. Lot, in Peter's authoritative reading, was 'greatly distressed by the sensual conduct of the wicked' and was righteous in this standpoint (2 Pet. 2:7). What happened in Sodom, then, was not primarily a failure to be neighborly. The men of Sodom turned away from God's good design for human sexuality. They indulged 'in the lust of defiling passion' and occasioned God's wrath because of it (2 Pet. 2:10). Sodom and Gomorrah function in the biblical mind as a terrible warning about what will happen to those who do not turn from the sin of homosexuality and trust Christ as Savior.

The Witness of the Levitical Law

Just as it does about opposite-sex lust, the Bible speaks with one voice about homosexuality. As we move forward in the biblical chronology, we see that Leviticus addresses same-sex behavior as well. The law for the old covenant people of God addresses homosexuality as one of several perverse practices, as Leviticus 18:19-23 shows.

> You shall not approach a woman to uncover her nakedness while she is in her menstrual uncleanness. And you shall not lie sexually with your neighbor's wife and so make yourself unclean with her. You shall not give any of your children to offer them to Molech, and so profane the name of your God: I am the Lord. You shall not lie with a male as with a woman; it is an abomination. And you shall not lie with any animal and so make yourself unclean with it, neither shall any woman give herself to an animal to lie with it: it is perversion.

Sleeping 'with a male as with a woman' is no light and glancing act (v. 22). It is *toebah*, or 'abomination.' Abominatory practices in the Scripture are practices that, generally speaking, not only signal sin against God's will, but sin against God's design. In other words, what is labeled 'abomination' in the Old Testament is not arbitrary. Such behaviors are doubly offensive to God, for they offend both

God's decree (His command) and His design.[12] Homosexuality is one of several such perversions, and in levitical terms is grouped amongst child sacrifice and bestiality (sex with an animal).

This passage explicitly teaches us that sin offends God in His nature. In other words, when we do wrong things, we are not only breaking a certain code of conduct, bad as that is. When we do wrong things, we are offending God Himself. We are personally *wronging* God. This is not, we know, the normal way to talk about sin of most any kind. At a basic level, we naturally think of sin as *stuff we shouldn't do because it's not nice.* That's true – but sin is actually more than that. Sin is us shaking our fist at God. We don't sin out of an innocent heart and good intentions; we sin because we have a sinful nature, a nature that is opposed to God, a nature that actually hates God (Rom. 3:10-18).[13]

---

12 John Kleinig speaks to the polluting nature of this behavior: 'This term is used in Leviticus for sexual practices that defile the people engaging in them, as well as defiling their environment. This eventually leads to God withdrawing his presence from people.' John W. Kleinig, *Leviticus*, Concordia Commentary (Saint Louis, MO: Concordia Pub. House, 2003), p. 379.

13 We note that this is true even when we are not necessarily aware of the offensive nature of our sin. Sometimes we are, to be sure, but sometimes we are not. As a biblical demonstration of this principle, we think of how

This is all generally true in biblical terms. We cannot miss, though, that some sins cause God special offense. Some sins He especially hates. When the Israelites acted like other ancient peoples and sacrificed their children to false gods, God detested those practices. When the people of God embraced wicked sexuality and engaged in homosexual acts, God called this behavior 'abomination.' So, to bring all this together: all sin offends God personally, but some sin especially angers Him, for it violates His holy design.

This tells us that we cannot do whatever we want with our bodies. We cannot simply follow whatever sexual desire courses within us to its logical end. We will develop this point below, but for now we note very simply that the Old Testament plainly tells the Israelites, God's people, to *not* act on ungodly desires. Homosexual sexual activity is blasphemy against God. It is outlawed in the moral code of Israel. It is part of a broader pattern of behavior that is driven not by holiness, but by conformity to sin. Elsewhere in the levitical law, we learn that this behavior deserves the death penalty, as do adultery, familial polgyamy, and bestiality (Lev. 20:10-16). Here again, we face a great

---

priests offered atoning sacrifices for sins committed in ignorance (see Lev. 5:17-18, for example).

and sobering reality: no person meets God's holy standard. All stand in desperate need of His grace.

The Declaration of Jesus in Matthew 19

As we move to the New Testament, we see that Jesus Christ, the center of all Scripture and history, reinforces the teaching we have covered thus far. In Matthew 19:3-6, He answers a question about divorce from the Pharisees who seek to entrap Him. In doing so, He tells us explicitly what He affirmed about sexuality:

> And Pharisees came up to him and tested him by asking, 'Is it lawful to divorce one's wife for any cause?' He answered, 'Have you not read that he who created them from the beginning made them male and female, and said, "Therefore a man shall leave his father and his mother and hold fast to his wife, and the two shall become one flesh"? So they are no longer two but one flesh. What therefore God has joined together, let not man separate.'

We sometimes hear that Jesus never said anything about homosexuality. While it is true that He does not *technically* speak explicitly about it here, it is also true that He teaches that God's creation design is good, beautiful, and righteous. Jesus quotes and upholds Genesis 2:24 in Matthew 19. The original plan of God for marriage and the family needs no updating in the Son of

God's mind. For Jesus, the Old Testament is not a substandard book from ancient times that has no relevance anymore. For Jesus, the Old Testament decrees what marriage is: it is a covenant, an unbreakable covenant, of one man who leaves his family and creates a new one with his wife. Sexual union in marriage is, just as Moses taught in Genesis 2, honorable before the Lord. 'One flesh' coming together brings no shame and breaks no law in Christ's mind.

By contrast, all other visions of sexuality fall short in Christ's mind. There is no new way to marry or enjoy sex or produce children. The Son of God upholds and affirms the good creational design of Genesis 2. This is remarkable, for it shows us that even though the fall of Genesis 3 destabilizes the world, yet God's wise plan for marriage holds steady. Jesus here has the chance to revise things if He wishes, but He has no such desire. He instead wants His hearers to understand that God's ways are best.

This is true of homosexuality. It is true of any thinking that would lead us to believe that there is any way to glorify God in sexual terms outside of covenantal marriage. There is not. Marriage is not dependent on or driven by our feelings. Sexuality is not an instinct to be expressed however our heart desires. The Scripture teaches us that God has a good plan, a righteous design, for all human people. If we are called to marriage, it is one man – one woman union that pleases and honors the Lord. No other sexual involvement or arrangement carries the blessing of God and His Son.

Here we come to understand better why the Bible says little about polygamy and some other perverse forms of sexuality. We should not read Scripture as endorsing anything it does not condemn. Instead, we should always strive to understand the biblical ideal for a holy life, and work outwards from there. Here's what I mean: while neither the OT nor the NT explicitly disavow polygamy (marriage to numerous people), it's exquisitely clear in both testaments that God is glorified by one man marrying one woman. This is what we learn in Genesis 2:24 from the world's earliest days; this is what we hear in Matthew 19:3-6 from the Son of God.

These can admittedly be tricky matters to address. Christians today often get the polygamy objection mentioned above in apologetic and evangelistic conversations. Smart skeptics sometimes argue that the Bible's 'silence' on polygamy shows that it actually endorses or leaves moral room for polygamy, a clever point. Yet the Bible, as we are seeing, is not 'silent' on polygamy. It addresses it implicitly in many places. God's vision for holy sexuality is from start to finish grounded in complementary marriage, and all else falls short. If God wanted to approve of polygamy, He would have, but the biblical authors inspired by His Spirit to write the Word of God nowhere do (though some biblical figures sin by marrying numerous people).

We could say it this way: God is not giving us in Scripture the option for sexuality He prefers, while also offering us any number of other choices. To the contrary, when God tells us His will for us, He is communicating what is good and right and holy and joy-giving and honorable. God does not confuse us in the Bible by listing His primary interest while leaving numerous other options undiscussed. He does not drop hints, in other words, and hope we'll pick them up. God is a clear communicator. God is a perfect communicator. When He tells us that His good plan for human sexuality is covenantal marriage, He has no alternatives in mind.

In applying this principle to Christ's own speech in Matthew 19, we see that there is no righteous outlet for human sexuality outside of covenantal marriage. Our sinful hearts must fight all manner of ungodly identities, thoughts, desires, and actions.[14] We have all strayed from God's good ways, and we must all confess and repent of sin on a regular basis even as believers. We are no perfect people. However, we are the people who seek by God's kindness to live according to God's good will, a moral plan for our lives introduced in the Old Testament and upheld (and extended) by Jesus in the New Testament.

The Teaching of Romans 1 on Paganism and Fallen Sexuality

We move to one final textual place in the Bible: Romans 1:18-32. In this lengthy passage, the Apostle Paul gives the Scripture's most extended treatment of God-defying sexuality. Paul does not limit his comments to only one dimension of

---

14 This includes 'unwanted' sins that pop up in our hearts. Hear John Owen on this count: 'I know no greater burden in the life of a believer than these involuntary surprisals of soul; involuntary, I say, as to the actual consent of the will, but not so in respect of that corruption which is in the will, and is the principle of them.' John Owen, 'The Nature, Power, Deceit, and Prevalency of the Remainders of Indwelling Sin in Believers,' in *The Works of John Owen*, vol. 6, *Temptation and Sin* (Edinburgh: Banner of Truth, 1967), pp. 153-322; cited in Denny Burk and Heath Lambert, *Transforming Homosexuality: What the Bible Says about Sexual Orientation and Change* (Phillipsburg, New Jersey: P&R, 2015), p. 122.

sexual sin, but rather weaves a true narrative of defiance, depravity, and damnation as the state of fallen humanity. We will quote this material at length in order to take it all in and best understand it, sobering and counter-cultural as it is.

> For the wrath of God is revealed from heaven against all ungodliness and unrighteousness of men, who by their unrighteousness suppress the truth. For what can be known about God is plain to them, because God has shown it to them. For his invisible attributes, namely, his eternal power and divine nature, have been clearly perceived, ever since the creation of the world, in the things that have been made. So they are without excuse. For although they knew God, they did not honor him as God or give thanks to him, but they became futile in their thinking, and their foolish hearts were darkened. Claiming to be wise, they became fools, and exchanged the glory of the immortal God for images resembling mortal man and birds and animals and creeping things.
>
> Therefore God gave them up in the lusts of their hearts to impurity, to the dishonoring of their bodies among themselves, because they exchanged the truth about God for a lie and worshiped and served the creature rather than the Creator, who is blessed forever! Amen.
>
> For this reason God gave them up to dishonorable passions. For their women exchanged natural rela-

tions for those that are contrary to nature; and the men likewise gave up natural relations with women and were consumed with passion for one another, men committing shameless acts with men and receiving in themselves the due penalty for their error.

And since they did not see fit to acknowledge God, God gave them up to a debased mind to do what ought not to be done. They were filled with all manner of unrighteousness, evil, covetousness, malice. They are full of envy, murder, strife, deceit, maliciousness. They are gossips, slanderers, haters of God, insolent, haughty, boastful, inventors of evil, disobedient to parents, foolish, faithless, heartless, ruthless. Though they know God's righteous decree that those who practice such things deserve to die, they not only do them but give approval to those who practice them.

This passage gives us the Bible's clearest concise sketch of the worldview that directly opposes God's design. The spiral of sin traced in Romans 1:18-32 begins in a familiar place: thanklessness to God (v. 21). We human people naturally know about God's 'eternal power' and 'divine nature,' and so are not confused about His existence.

But though we can clearly identify divine power and existence in the created world, we deny these realities in our sin. We should give praise to the Creator, but we do not. He deserves our total worship and unquestioning love, yet we defy Him, refusing to thank Him for all His common grace gifts: life, health, friends, family, provision, and so on. Because of this, our thinking, Paul teaches, becomes 'futile,' and our heart becomes 'darkened' (v. 21). This means that we will never be able to think God's thoughts after Him; we use the brain given to us to know God to dwell on lesser things, and even to try to disprove God Himself.

In this terrible state—truly our natural sinful condition—we make two awful swaps. We 'exchange' God's glory for creaturely glory and we 'exchange' God's truth for a creaturely lie (vv. 23, 25). What a concise yet devastating summary of human sinfulness this is. Though God's glory is dazzling and deserving of never-ending attention, we disdain it. We choose to focus on the things created by God rather than our Creator. Though God's truth frames the world rightly, putting everything into proper perspective and order, we reject it. We choose our own truth instead, believing the lie that we can function as God. Our view, not God's revelation, matters most. This decision of the mind and heart effectively silences God. We do not want to hear from Him; we do not want His correction; we do not wish to hear His call to repentance.

This sums up the human condition, doesn't it? Before we get to Paul's discussion of sinful sexuality, we see that Paul's understanding of our problem is much wider than a mere momentary choice. Our sin is grounded in our defiance of God, our rebellion against Him, our trust of ourselves over the Creator. We would rather do *anything* but offer God praise and worship and humble repentance. We are wired by our sin to do everything but submit to God.

The end result of this sorry chain is that the pagans end up worshiping and serving the creature (v. 25). Though they should see only God as glorious, they elevate the body—that of creatures and fellow human beings—to a position of glory. They become creature-worshippers. This leads to the issue of homosexuality: enmeshed in idolatry, men and women alike give up on 'natural relations' with the opposite sex in the covenant of marriage (vv. 26-7). They give up on 'nature' itself as verse 26 makes clear; Paul means by this term that in such sexual encounters (and self-identity) the pagans cease to follow the design of God.

So we see that rebellion comes full circle. The pagans are not only straying from God's path, but are acting out their wickedness without check. R. C. Sproul puts the matter in stark terms: '[Paul] sees the sin of homosexual behavior as the sin most representative of the radical nature of our fall. It is seen here not simply as a sin, nor even as a serious sin or a gross sin, but as the clearest expression of the depths of our perversity.'[15] It is crucial that we understand this point, offensive as it is to modern ears. In embracing homosexuality, sinners make for themselves their own design; said differently, they re-design what God has already designed. Their rebellion is complete.[16]

The pagans deny the natural complementarity of the male and female body, and so create a new sexual order. Men lie with men, and women lie with women. In doing so, they offend God's will and God's good design. They dishonor the Lord with their substitute sexuality. God is not unaware of this shift. He gives sinners up to 'dishonorable passions' (v. 26). This is not all: He also gives them up to 'a debased mind' (v. 28). The relationship of destructive 'giving'—begun in verse 24—concludes in verse 32, where we learn that the Gentiles 'give

---

15 R. C. Sproul, *Romans* (Wheaton, IL: Crossway, 2009), p. 51.

16 This is a place of terrifying isolation from God. The people who embrace such behavior, whether at the local or territorial or national level (or some such), are far from the Lord. Yet we need to make clear as well that as powerful as this unimpeded debauchery is, still the gospel saves sinners to the uttermost. No one can outrun the Lord. No one is unsaveable. Praise God for this truth!

approval' to those who contravene God's righteous decree.[17] Those who are given over to their sin go on to give approval to those who disobey God.

This disobedience takes many forms, of course; all sin blasphemes God, all sin occasions God's just wrath, all sin separates us from God by an infinite gap. Yet we must not miss the course of destruction the Gentiles travel according to Romans 1. They do not only sample different iniquities, Paul teaches, but rather replace biblical sexuality with pagan sexuality. Homosexuality is not merely one outgrowth of this replacement; it is the sign that both God's will and God's design have been decisively rejected by men and women. Genesis 2 is lost. Genesis 2 is scorned. Sodom's sin is embraced. The people who have done this give approval to those who join them in this rebellion.

What we need to see at this point is this: we are not sinners in the sense that once in a while we do something messed up. We are not only broken.

---

17 This is called 'judicial abandonment' by the Reformed tradition. See John Murray: 'God's displeasure is expressed in his abandonment of the persons concerned to more intensified and aggravated cultivation of the lusts of their own hearts with the result that they reap for themselves a correspondingly greater toll of retributive vengeance.' John Murray, *The Epistle to the Romans*, vol. 1, The New International Commentary on the Old and New Testament (Grand Rapids, MI; Cambridge, U.K.: Wm. B. Eerdmans Publishing Co., 1968), pp. 44-5.

We do not only wander. Romans 1 tells us, to the contrary, that we are depraved, haters of God, and rebellious to the core. We have dynamited the design of God and created nothing less than a new order. We call this new order 'paganism,' or more accurately for our time, 'neo-paganism.' (This means 'new' paganism.) What is paganism, you ask? Paganism is the anti-wisdom of the serpent which deconstructs ordered reality—the God-made world—and replaces it with a new order, an anti-order ruled by the devil. In this anti-order, there is no biblical God; no divine design; no male or female; no script for sexuality; no God-designed family with a father, mother, and children; no need to protect and care for children at all; no Savior, Lord, or theistic end to the cosmos; and no judge of evil.

The theologian Peter Jones calls this 'one-ism,' signifying that paganism reduces everything to sameness. Jones argues that 'one-ism' is basically 'nature worship.' In this system, 'there's no category for sin, because think of a circle, everything is within the circle, rocks, trees, good and evil, man and God. Everything is one, and so in that circle, we can do whatever we want to.'[18] This is a strikingly different worldview than biblical Christianity, in which the

---

18 Peter Jones, 'After Darkness, Light,' 2015 Ligonier Conference Message, accessible at https://www.ligonier.org/learn/conferences/after-darkness-light-2015-national-

Creator and the creature are distinct.[19] Everything is not one; there is God, and there is everything else.

Pulling it All Together: The Sinfulness of Homosexuality

This discussion has major relevance for the subject of this text. In pagan terms, when we reject God we will also reject His design. We will reinvent gender and marriage, making each whatever we desire them to be, while expressing 'tolerance for all religions' and 'all lifestyles' as Jones notes. In cultural and societal terms, we will rework everything about our humanity. A pagan people distrusts hard-and-fast morality, downplays absolute truth, holds a self-generating view of existence and cosmological origins, believes that spirituality is a matter of internal alignment rather than external obeisance, sees redemption as a project of self-actualization ('I want to be my best self') and the self as a little god (in different

---

conference/paganism-in-todays-culture. Last accessed January 2020.

19 This is called the Creator-creature distinction, and it is very important in theology and ethics. God is God; we are not. It is not just God is way bigger than us; it is that He is not us, and we are not Him. We are fully dependent on Him. See Cornelius Van Til, *The Intellectual Challenge of the Gospel* (Phillipsburg, NJ: Presbyterian and Reformed Publishing Co., 1980), p. 19.

forms), and finds no higher purpose in death and the trajectory of the cosmos.

Do these 'values' and practices sound familiar? They should. Many of us find ourselves in contexts that are increasingly neo-pagan and decreasingly traditional (let alone biblical in any way). We need to know what we face today, and what we face is not so much a few isolated challenges, but a worldview, a system, a full-orbed philosophy that disenchants our humanity and re-envisions our identity. A key part of this system is homosexuality, which is the rejection of God's good plan for personal holiness, manhood or womanhood, marriage, and the family. Whether we've read a single page of a pagan author or not, homosexuality is a counterfeit sexuality in line with a serpentine spirituality.

By identifying this system as we have, we do not mean that every person who battles same-sex attraction (SSA) lights candles each night to a neo-pagan goddess. No doubt—as we have said previously—a good number of people experience SSA and are confused by it; many would rather not have it. But they do not know what to do about SSA, and further, they are told at every turn by a non-Christian culture that SSA is not only good, but the very marker of their identity. What compassion we have for people in such circumstances. But lest we miscontrue them and us, they are not innocent; they are not victims. Like all of us, they are complicit in their sin given their sin nature, their sin welling up from within. Think of what theologian Charles Hodge once wrote about both 'deliberate' and 'impulsive' sins, all of which come from a depraved heart:

> We do attribute moral character to principles which precede all voluntary action and which are entirely independent of the power of the will.... We hold ourselves responsible not only for the deliberate acts of the will, that is, for acts of deliberate self-determination, which suppose both knowledge and volition, but also for emotional, impulsive acts, which precede all deliberation; and not only for such impulsive acts, but also for the principles, dispositions, or immanent states of the mind, by which its acts whether impulsive or deliberate, are determined.[20]

These words ring out with piercing clarity in our age. Christian love should motivate us to tell fellow sinners of every kind of the freedom found not in worldly affirmation and ungodly lusts, but in confession and repentance of all sin in the name of

---

20 Charles Hodge, *Systematic Theology* (New York: Charles Scribner, 1872; repr., Peabody, MA: Hendrickson, 1999), p. 2:107; cited in Burk and Lambert, *Transforming Homosexuality*, pp. 31-2.

Christ. To speak the truth in love, we must calmly and compassionately say the following in line with Hodge's general summary of sin: Homosexuality is sinful. This is true at every level: homosexual identity, homosexual thinking, homosexual desires, homosexual actions. There is no part of homosexuality that the Bible sanctifies and calls holy. There is no part of homosexuality that we can distinguish as good. There is no part of homosexuality that a Christian can embrace. There is no part of homosexuality that is a 'neutral' or praiseworthy part of our identity or experience.

In biblical terms, we have seen that the scriptural authors speak with one voice. They do not commend homosexuality in any form; they warn against it in the strongest terms. When a person experiences SSA, then, they should repent. This is not a new plan for only one type of sinner; this is what every person should do when an ungodly thought, desire, or action crops up in their life.[21] It is not the intensity or length

---

21 This is also an ancient practice. In the early fifth century, Augustine preached the following: 'And so it is that if we desire to receive pardon, we must be ready to pardon all wrongs committed against us. After all, if we take a look at our own sins, and try counting what we commit by deed, with our eyes, with our ears, in our thoughts, by innumerable impulses ...' Augustine, 'Sermon 83,' in *Sermons 51-94*, vol. 3 of Part III – *Sermons, The Works of*

of the thought, desire, or action that demands repentance; it is the wrongness of these things, their *telos* (end). By extension, we cannot make room for homosexuality in our identity, either; we must reject a 'gay Christian' self-conception and anything like it.

Even as we outline the dimensions of a faithful battle with SSA, we cannot miss the white comet of hope that courses through the biblical storyline. No sinner is unreachable. No one is beyond God's saving grasp. All people have dignity and worth as image-bearers, and all people have hope as those God can save. As we shall see in our next chapter, the gospel is more powerful than any sin, and Christ loves to save sinners of every kind. To that powerful gospel, and that loving Christ, we now turn.

Saint Augustine: A Translation for the 21st Century, ed. John E. Rotelle (Brooklyn: New City Press, 1997), p. 381; cited in Jared Moore, 'A Biblical and Historical Appraisal of Same-Sex Attraction,' PhD Thesis, The Southern Baptist Theological Seminary, 2019, p. 38.

2. THE TRANSFORMING POWER OF THE GOSPEL

As we have seen, God has nothing less than divine disdain for anything that opposes that purpose in nature as He intended. In other words, anything that goes against complementary unity, complementary polarity (distinctiveness), complementary reciprocity, complementary interest and complementary desire for marriage is un-natural. Therefore, it is anti-God. It is Satan's anti-wisdom. It is neo-paganism.

But why, if this is true, does Paul give particular attention to homosexuality in Romans 1 verses 24-27 and only give a mere mention to the multitude of other sins in verses 29-31? The answer is surely that complementary sexuality in a marriage was made in creation to be a picture of God's love in redemption. Neo-pagan behavior of the homosexual kind does not allow the display of union that Paul shows us in Ephesians 5:31-2:

Therefore a man shall leave his father and mother and hold fast to his wife, and the two shall become *one flesh. This mystery is profound, and I am saying that **it refers to Christ and the church**.*

Here Paul is citing Genesis 2:24 and God's pre-fall creation institution of marriage between man and woman. He says that this is a 'mystery' that refers to Christ and the church. A 'mystery' is something that was hidden to a certain extent in the past. And Paul says this mystery is now being made clear. It is the mystery of one man united in all senses with one woman in loving covenant, a mystery that culminates in Christ's love for His Bride. It is this mystery, the point of human sexuality, that homosexuality obscures.[1]

The Dismantling of Marriage

In this passage Paul is communicating that this 'holding fast,' the one flesh union of marriage, is a picture of the covenant love of Christ for His church. It is a picture of the divine drama of the gospel. That's the link between the gospel and the marriage of a man to a woman. John Piper says it elegantly in his book, *This Momentary Marriage*:

Christ obtained the church by His blood and formed a new covenant with her, an unbreakable

---

1   In truth, homosexuality corrupts sex, creating a bodily encounter that is not 'union' in creational terms, and that thus cannot display the mystery of husband-wife oneness, a oneness that is truly spiritual in the case of Christ and His church.

'marriage.' *The ultimate thing we can say about marriage is that it exists for God's glory. That is, it exists to display God ...* Now we see how: Marriage is patterned after Christ's covenant relationship to His redeemed people, the church. And therefore, the highest meaning and the most ultimate purpose of marriage is to put the covenant relationship of Christ and His church on display. That is why marriage exists ... *Staying married, therefore, is not mainly about staying in love. It is about keeping covenant ... It is about showing in real life the glory of the gospel.*[2]

Piper's words ring true. Manhood and womanhood and how we use our sexuality accordingly is swept up into the greatest reality of the glory of God. That is the glory of His grace in sending His Son to die for sinners (Eph. 1:6). Moreover, the sexual union between a man and a woman in marriage directs us to the union of Christ and the church.[3] Though we must make clear that the mystical union of Christ and the church is not sexual, our sexuality expressed in sexual union in marriage is

---

2   John Piper, *This Momentary Marriage* (Downers Grove, Illinois: InterVarsity, 2009), p. 25-26.

3   As noted in Chapter 1: creational norms (including marriage) point us to the fulfillment found in the new creation, which culminates in the marriage of Christ and His church at the end of the age.

connected to a spiritual reality that is far greater than the earthly picture.

Therefore, all sexual immorality mars and blurs the picture of this gospel reality. Heterosexual adultery is a parable of spiritual adultery, but homosexuality is a further departure from the gospel picture. So we could say that if the joining of a man and woman in marriage is a portrait of the church's relationship to God, the homosexual act is a vivid portrayal of a broken relationship with God and a jarring rebellion against God's design for His glory in male and female image bearers. We can also add that same-sex sex is in fact a clear picture of self-love. It is a devastating dismantling of marriage.

As we think about this it is helpful to recognize some historical landmarks in the sexual revolution that we have seen over the past half a century. In 2013 a bill was passed in England and Wales to legalize 'same-sex marriage' and the first took place in March 2014. The USA followed suit in 2015 with the Supreme Court legalizing it in all fifty states. It is currently available in twenty-eight countries worldwide, including South Africa, Colombia, and Ireland.

But we didn't just arrive at 'same-sex marriage' out of the blue. How then did we land here? It has been a subtle process. We have gradually normalized homosexuality and slowly become desensitized to its sinfulness. This has been enabled by a move in our language to describe it. As little as fifty years ago sex between two men was described by the un-natural action: 'sodomy.' In the 1980s it was categorized as a psychological disorder: 'homosexuality.' And in recent years it has been termed as an identity: 'gay.' In describing same-sex sexuality we have moved from an action to a psychological condition to an identity.

Once the surrounding culture accepted homosexuality as an identity the number of practicing homosexuals increased substantially. Because individual feelings trump objective truth, and homosexual feelings are considered a natural identity, it is now considered repressive to say no to such feelings. As a result, the holy creation institution of marriage between one man and one woman as the only place for sexual union has been gradually dismantled. In addition to this, there have been other markers along the way. With the introduction of the Pill you can have sex without the consequence of a baby. This, alongside the creation of no-fault divorce, facilitated the normalcy of cohabitation rather than lifelong commitment in complementary marriage. IVF introduced another possibility (granted, it is used with different aims in view). With the Pill (and now legalized abortion) you could have sex without babies. With IVF technology you could have babies without sex. All the time the normalization of homosexuality was gradually increasing so that as marriage became more redundant, the culture was more ready to accept a redefinition of marriage. Enter the legalization of gay marriage into a culture of neo-paganism (as we saw in Chapter 1).[4]

Whereas God created sex for the covenant of marriage and the potential of babies, now we have a culture where the only thing you need for sex is consent, and although you still need a sperm and an egg you don't need a married man and woman to unite in a sexual union in order to produce babies. This has opened the door for gay 'married' couples to adopt so that children today are being taught an anti-biblical, anti-traditional view of family.[5]

Power Greater Than Our Sin: The Witness of 1 Corinthians 6

Nevertheless, there is nothing new under the sun and the Holy Scriptures are sufficient for our

---

4   Albert Mohler expands on the timeline and markers along the way that led to the legalization of same-sex marriage in his book *We Must Not Be Silent*.

5   Tragically, this neo-pagan family is not in truth a family; nothing can be a family but what God designs.

interpretation of our times. In the early church in Corinth they were struggling to depart from ancient paganism and fleshliness, including homosexuality. We now turn to Paul's specific address to a church that had been influenced by the Corinthian culture around them.

> Or do you not know that the unrighteous will not inherit the kingdom of God? Do not be deceived: neither the sexually immoral, nor idolaters, nor adulterers, nor men who practice homosexuality, nor thieves, nor the greedy, nor drunkards, nor revilers, nor swindlers will inherit the kingdom of God. And such were some of you. But you were washed, you were sanctified, you were justified in the name of the Lord Jesus Christ and by the Spirit of our God (1 Cor. 6:9-11).

To 'live like a Corinthian' was to live a life of sexual immorality and deviancy and all kinds of hedonistic pleasure-seeking.[6] Sexual immorality, adultery, and homosexuality marked the culture. How similar this is to our licentious day! However, the

---

6   The Corinthians famously worshiped Aphrodite, the goddess of love, and 'Her temple on the Acrocorinthus had more than a thousand hierodouloi – priestesses of vice [temple prostitutes] not found in other shrines of Greece, and she attracted worshipers from all over the ancient world.' J. D. Douglas and Merrill C. Tenney, *The New International Dictionary of the Bible* (Grand Rapids: Zondervan Academic, 1987), p. 233.

gospel had broken into Corinth and people were being saved and gathered into the local church. But as is the case for every Christian in any age they needed warning and instruction about their new identity and ethical responsibilities. Even more relevant to our discussion is that some of the Corinthian church had been characterized by a homosexual lifestyle. For a moment just notice Paul's words in verse 11, 'And such were some of you' (1 Cor. 6:11).

At this stage we should briefly pause to consider this hopeful phrase. You may be reading this book and looking for help to overcome a homosexual lifestyle or feeling guilty as you experience sexual feelings for a member of the same sex. Or maybe you are simply seeking to understand how the gospel addresses homosexuality. Suffice to say there is great hope in Paul's words, 'And such *were* some of you.' Paul acknowledges that there were some in the congregation who had habitually engaged in homosexual behavior. But this was not and could not be who they were anymore.

Clearly sexual immorality was happening in the visible body of the church. Paul had dealt with this in chapter 5 with the command to excommunicate the man who slept with his father's wife (1 Cor. 5:1-2). Perhaps there were Christians in the Corinthian church who had been genuinely saved but still experienced the pull of same-sex desire or were dabbling in the pagan sexuality to which they once belonged. The text does not say explicitly. But as we have established in Book One of this trilogy, *What Does the Bible Say About Lust?*, we must not only repent of sinful acts but also of sinful desires.[7] And there is no homosexual action without homosexual desire preceding it. If it is sinful to do it, it is sinful to desire it.[8]

Nevertheless, there is hope for doing-and-desiring sinners like us. In these words, 'And such were some of you' is the proclamation that the gospel has the power to save and transform people from the inside out: from something they were to something they are. The effect is that the Corinthians can and must engage in a pure lifestyle that involves fighting homosexual desires and homosexual actions. We will return to this in a moment but it is important to sound this note of hope as we look at the warning of judgment that Paul begins with in 1 Corinthians 6:9-11.

---

7 We covered this material fully in Book One of this trilogy – see Chapter 2.

8 We must also make clear that there are different kinds of temptation in Scripture: there is internal temptation and external temptation of the kind Christ faced in Matthew 4:1-11. For more on this tricky point, see Chapter 2 of Book One (also Strachan, *Reenchanting Humanity*, pp. 347-84.

A Divine Warning

I used to love to kick my football (soccer ball) around in my back garden. Now and then, however, I would kick it over the fence and into the next-door neighbor's property. My skills were clearly not perfected! There were two signs in the garden: 'Trespassers Will Be Prosecuted' and 'Beware of the Dog.' These were warnings to keep off the land, with the threat of a consequence from the owner or his vicious dog if the warning was ignored. Warnings are designed to get our attention and divert us from a course of action, the penalty for which will not be pleasant. Often warnings offend our personal sense of justice and entitlement and we think, 'Why not?' I certainly did. I only wanted to get my ball back. I didn't want to wait to ask the owner when he returned home. But good sense prevailed as I weighed the consequences of a clip round the ear or a dog bite on the backside! I heeded the warning.

We cannot miss that Paul starts with a divine warning in our passage:

> Or do you not know that the unrighteous will not inherit God's kingdom? (1 Cor. 6:9).

He goes on to elaborate by telling them not to be deceived and that the unrighteous include those who are unrepentant of homosexuality (1 Cor. 6:9).

We must not ignore this warning. Alongside all the unrighteous—those who have not repented of their sins and been forgiven through faith in Jesus Christ—the homosexual will stand, excluded from heaven. Homosexuality is unrighteous. We have already seen that the Bible consistently maintains the sinfulness of homosexuality in both the Old and New Testaments. In addition, here in 1 Corinthians we have an explicit statement about the consequence of homosexuality. If a person does not turn from it they will not inherit the kingdom; in other words, they will not enter the kingdom of heaven but will stay under God's wrath for eternity in Hell.

Homosexuality is part of sexual immorality and departs from the only place for sexual acting, thinking, speaking and touching; that is complementary marriage. But it is also interesting that in this passage Paul indicts both the passive and active roles of the homosexual encounter where he writes in verse 9, 'men who practice homosexuality' (*oute malakoi oute arsenokoitai*). Some say that these words should be only treated as meaning prostitution or pederasty (adult males who have sex with boys). The argument here says that only those who engage in homosexual acts in exploitive relationships are in view. It would, therefore, allow for consensual long-term loving relationships between two men, for instance. Proponents of this argument say that those men could be Christian and enter the kingdom. Is this true?

Let us look at the two words for a moment. 'Arsenokoites' literally means 'bedders of men' – *arsen* (men), *koites* (bed). It refers to the male who penetrates his male partner. Paul's use of the word refers back to the Levitical holiness code in 18:22 and 20:13, which when translated in the Greek Septuagint uses the same word:

Leviticus 18:22, 'you shall not lie with a male as with a woman'
*Meta **arsenos** ou koimethese **koiten** gynaikos*

Leviticus 20:13, 'whoever shall lie with a male as with a woman'
*Hos an koimethe meta **arsenos koiten** gynaikos*

This discussion gets technical pretty quickly, as you can tell. But here's the point you shouldn't miss: Paul's words, like the words of Leviticus, speak to homosexuality directly. Some argue that Paul had in mind only exploitative same-sex relationships in the Roman world, where a man would use a boy for his sexual pleasure, for example. But if Paul wanted to target that sin alone, he would have used the word for pederasty (*paiderastes*) or prostitution (*pornes*). You may not get a PhD in Greek, but here's what you should know: Paul condemns homosexuality in the broadest terms. In other words, there is no appropriate expression of homosexuality. Whatever the age, whatever the background of sexual partners, this expression of sexuality is wrong, hard as this biblical word is for some.

Paul does not make this point simply by asserting it. As we have seen, he grounds his argument in the broader Old Testament sexual ethic. This ethic is itself rooted in creation order, and affirmed in the Ten Commandments and the Levitical holiness code. In the pagan culture of ancient Rome a man would be considered manly if he had sex with his wife, a prostitute of either sex, or a young boy (pederasty). As long as he was the active partner it was okay. But the Bible affirms the creation order and goodness of sex between a man and a woman in marriage alone. Arsenokoites is against God's design and Paul clearly condemns it.

The second word Paul uses in the text in 1 Corinthians is *malakoi*, meaning 'soft ones' or 'effeminate.' This refers to the passive partner in the sexual relationship between two men. But is this all it means? We will now briefly consider a very important point about homosexuality and biblical manhood. Whilst *malakoi* certainly means the effeminate one in the homosexual encounter it must also include effeminate behavior. Listen to John Calvin's words on 1 Cor. 6:9: 'By effeminate persons I understand those who, although they do not openly abandon themselves to impurity, discover, nevertheless, their unchastity by blandishments of speech, by lightness of gesture and apparel, and other allurements.'[9] This is old-fashioned language, but here's what it means. Calvin denounces effeminacy of behavior in general, not just in the bedroom. He teaches that effeminacy effectively banishes one from the kingdom. This is a chilling warning.

We Should Not Be Effeminate Men (nor Manly Women)

Why is effeminate behavior sinful? (We'll ask that question first because of the text, and then think about what we call 'manly womanhood.') The answer is firstly that condemning the homosexual act, but not effeminate behavior, is an accommodation which indirectly attacks God's design of binary sexes. Failing to call out effeminacy means that the problem is not substantially addressed. If we fall into this trap, we will not appreciate God's design, which

---

9   Calvin's Commentaries, Vol. XX, *1 Corinthians, II Corinthians* (Grand Rapids: Baker, 2009), pp. 208-9.

includes—as we have argued earlier—what we call complementary unity, polarity, reciprocity, interest, and desire for marriage. The Bible, it turns out, is not at all indifferent to effeminacy (or manliness as embraced by women, which is equally un-natural). We'll say more in our third book of this trilogy; for now, consider this text: 'A woman shall not wear a man's garment, nor shall a man put on a woman's cloak, for whoever does these things is an abomination to the Lord your God.' (Deut. 22:5).

Secondly and subsequent to the first reason, is that if we allow for and affirm effeminate be-havior in a man we go against nature and ignore its teaching. John Piper says that nature 'inclines a man to feel repulsed and shameful about wearing culturally defined symbols of womanhood.'[10] This agrees with the Apostle Paul who says: 'Does not nature itself teach you that if a man wears long hair it is a disgrace for him?' (1 Cor. 11:14). Paul affirms here that it is un-natural for a man in Corinth to wear long hair. It goes against his created nature as male and violates God's good design by blurring or confusing the sexes. Remember that directly after Genesis 1:27 and God creating binary sexes,

---

10 Dr John Piper expresses this in the transcript of his *Ask Pastor John* podcast: https://www.desiringgod.org/interviews/is-it-wrong-for-men-to-have-long-hair. Last accessed January 2020.

male and female in His image, is the sex-related command to be fruitful and multiply in which the male and female have a different role that flows out of their created sex. We could say that gender behavior is directly related to, and controlled by, created sex. If you are a man you should act like a man. If you are a woman you should act like a woman. Nature teaches this.

In sum, effeminacy amongst men is an affront to manhood, and direct rebellion against God, His Word, and what He has designed in nature. Effeminacy in a man embraces the gender fluidity of our age. We see such behavior when men wear make-up, carry themselves in a womanly way, and speak with a nasally high-pitched voice. It is not something our current culture hides but rather seeks to promote. Just look around any shopping mall at many serving positions in the women's stores in those malls. We don't blush about these things anymore (Jer. 6:15). Our instincts and reflexes on sexuality have been dulled. Instead of being offended by effeminacy we are emotionally apathetic even if we consider it wrong. We have a less visceral response to effeminacy than we used to in the past.[11]

---

11 Effeminacy, of course, has been a part of entertainment culture for some time (shows like *I Love Lucy*). But this effeminacy was presented as humorous; it was not

As we make the case for the sinfulness of effeminate behavior as well as the effeminate homosexual sexual act it brings us back to the idea of the 'impulse' or 'reflex' that is contrary to nature. This is something that must be counted as sinful and in need of repentance, not just the act. This reflex does not only relate to effeminacy; while 1 Corinthians 6 and 11 indict men explicitly and most directly for their pagan gender-bending ways, we may also know that the Scripture gives no encouragement to what we could call 'manly womanliness.' Women should look distinct from men, as these passages show; women should exhibit a uniquely 'gentle and quiet spirit' (1 Pet. 3:4); women are encouraged to find real joy in nurture, domesticity, and helping others per Genesis 2, Proverbs 31, Titus 2, and other texts. There is no one hardline way to be a godly woman, to be sure; women have different personalities, heights, intelligence levels, interests, and so on. All of this is to God's glory. Yet women are called to be women, which is to say, distinct from men.[12]

---

presented as good or normal. Today, effeminacy and womanly manliness are presented as positive. This is because, ultimately, we live in a secular and neo-pagan culture that sees God-created 'nature' as a fiction.

12 Rick Holland, pastor of Mission Road Bible Church in Kansas City, has defined manhood and womanhood in

Maybe you are reading this book coming from a background where there has been no distinction between masculine and feminine behavior. This is now commonplace. Desensitization to the distinction between the sexes has led to demonic confusion. Satan loves confusion in God's design because it brings the destruction of God's glory in His image bearers and blurs the picture of the gospel in marriage.

Gay Is Good – Says the World

We have already looked at some of the historical landmarks along the way to the legalization of 'same-sex marriage' earlier in the chapter. But another of the contributing factors is that gay activists have been able to achieve more in a short space of time than women's rights or civil rights because as Linda Hirshman has noted, 'its leaders at critical points made the moral claim that "gay is good".'[13] They have made it a moral issue and

---

this way: Men are men in that they are neither a woman nor a boy; women are women in that they are neither a man nor a girl. Different cultures do express manhood and womanhood in unique ways; Christians in every culture seek to honor divine design in their particular context.

13 Linda Hirshman, *Victory: The Triumphant Gay Revolution/ How a Despised Minority Pushed Back, Beat Death, Found Love and Changed America for Everyone* (New York: Harper Collins, 2012), p. xvi.

therefore it became a civil rights issue. The moral claim then ushers in the social change. As Denny Burk has observed, because gay is established as morally good, the public cannot tolerate those who say it is not good. People who do not affirm this are called unkind, intolerant, immoral, and unloving people who hold society back.[14] Of course the lie that evil is good and good is evil has always been Satan's ploy from the beginning – he questioned the goodness of God and God's Word in Eden.

When a culture ignores God's Word and believes Satan's lie and remains stubbornly unrepentant God gives them over to rampant immorality. Listen to the Apostle Paul: 'Therefore God gave them up in the lusts of their hearts to impurity' (Rom. 1:24). He repeats this phrase 'God gave them up' twice more in the next verses. Then he concludes, 'Though they know God's righteous decree that those who practice such things deserve to die, they not only do them but give approval to those who practice them' (Rom. 1:32). If you are reading your Bible with one eye on the page and one eye on the culture, it is not difficult to see that we live in a society today

---

14 See Denny Burk, *What Is the Meaning of Sex?* (Wheaton, IL: Crossway, 2013), p. 187.

which God has given over to immorality so that we even approve of what is evil. The Bible says that all sexual same-sex relationships are sinful. But we live in an age of 'gay is good' and this is celebrated across the media and in many cities worldwide as the Rainbow flag is flown in the name of Gay Pride. We are seeing the moral approval of what is evil (see again Rom. 1:32).

If you are under thirty this is the water in which you have been swimming for much of your life. And this is why it feels acceptable to you – or at least not that bad. So we are aware that this book might make you feel uncomfortable, certainly if you are struggling with same-sex desire. Perhaps you are uncomfortable because you have gay family members, neighbors, work colleagues or school friends who are extremely nice people and you are being told that they are in deep sin and grave danger. Maybe you simply think it sounds harsh, unhelpful and unloving.

Certainly we do not wish to be insensitive to people's pain, loneliness and desires for happiness. Nor do we fail to confess—as we have done already in this book—that every person, however lost in sin, is nonetheless made in God's image and thus possessing great dignity and worth in ontological (essential) terms. But remember we have been looking at the words of the inspired apostle, Paul, who warns us in Holy Scripture that all homosexual behavior, whether any sexual relations occur or not, is sinfully out of step with God's design in creation and what He has instilled as natural to every man or woman. Homosexuality is actually not good for a person, even if they think it brings them immediate pleasure, because along with multiple other sins it will result in God's judgment. Paul warns us about this. Remember my illustration of the signs in the neighbor's garden. Warnings are designed to get our attention, are often jarring to our sensibilities, and might not seem comfortable to us initially.

You may feel those things after reading this section of the book. But remember this: Adam and Eve's failure to heed the warning of one 'No' in Eden because it didn't feel right led to the fall of man and every malady in the world today, including the immorality of homosexuality. Therefore, we conclude that it is pastorally loving and faithful to sound God's warnings in the right way. We need to let God's Word rewire our minds, actions and emotions. The purpose is to save people and bring glory to God and show people that as they live the way God created them to be they will be satisfied. This is our intention in this book.

So with Paul's divine warning having commanded our attention, we will now look at how the gospel changes us. We will see how faith in Jesus Christ as our Lord and Savior changes everything. And we will, I hope, celebrate how the Word of God realigns our minds and behavior to God's good purposes. As we continue to look at this passage from 1 Corinthians 6:9 onwards we will see that Paul explains this by reminding the Corinthian believers of their *spiritual identity* and their *bodily identity*.

The Christian's Spiritual Identity

As a young man I attended Bexley Grammar School in the South East London area. I remember getting dressed for that first morning at senior school (high school). I tied my tie, which showed off the school colors, and donned my blazer with the school badge with our motto emblazoned on it in Latin: *Praestantiae Studere* (Strive for Excellence). My parents then sent me off and exhorted me with these words, 'Remember who you are. When you are outside these walls you represent your family and your school. Don't forget to act like it.' Here was a sharp reminder of my identity as a member of the Peacock family and also a member of my new school. So there was a certain kind of family likeness and mature code of conduct that was now expected of me.

Paul is doing something like this with the Corinthians. He is reminding them of who they are as Christians and he tells them what Christian behavior looks like as a consequence. Amongst a list of unrighteous unrepentant sinners who will not enter heaven are the homosexuals, as we have already seen. And the first thing Paul says after he warns about their fate is, 'And such were some of you.' Not everyone in the church had been a homosexual, of course. But some had come out of that lifestyle which marked the prevailing pagan culture in Corinth. And Paul says to those believers, 'That is not you now. This style of life does not characterize you anymore. You have been dragged away from that and you do not represent that sin anymore.' He is saying that they have been converted to Christ now.

In his second letter to the Corinthians Paul expresses it like this: 'Therefore, if anyone is in Christ, he is a new creation. The old has passed away; behold, the new has come' (2 Cor. 5:17). What a thing! If you have trusted in Jesus Christ for the forgiveness of your sins you are a new creation! The 'old has passed away' is similar to saying 'and such were some of you.' Anyone who is in a gay relationship or who experiences same-sex attraction and then comes to Christ in faith has a new identity just like every other repentant sinner. If this is you, this is the reminder you need each day. We are all prone to spiritual amnesia. That's why we need spiritual warnings to awaken us and get our attention, but we also need spiritual reminders to instruct us on who we really are. Just as my parents reminded me of who I was before I left the house, Paul begins with a reminder to the Corinthians of who they are by saying who they are not.

You see, when you become a Christian you don't automatically stop sinning completely or cease to experience sinful passions. You might be a new creation but you are still living in a fallen world, in a fallen body with an unperfected soul. Some of the old habits of thoughts and lifestyle can still tempt you. You need reminding that the old ways are not yours anymore.

However, Paul insists that they cannot be half in Christ and half in Corinth. We need to state this clearly. This is why, with all due respect, we seek to dissuade readers from using the term 'Gay Christian.' That is an oxymoron. It is biblically untrue and pastorally unhelpful. It diverts a person away from their identity in Christ. It defines a Christian by sin for which Christ died. And it encourages them to think that it is okay to dwell in sexual feelings for the same sex simply because they are not acting upon them. Paul says, 'You cannot be defined by this anymore.' This includes the homosexual act. But we must also include the homosexual desire which causes the act.

So let's pause briefly to consider something here. Let's say you identify as a gay man or woman. You are in a same sex-relationship or maybe you are not in a relationship but you think you would like one because you experience sexual urges for the same sex. At the same time you are interested in Jesus. You have heard that He comes to seek and save the lost (Luke 19:10). If you listen to the Bible carefully in this chapter you will have seen that homosexuality is a grave sin, which destroys God's good plan of complementary, heterosexual marriage. You will have seen that the Bible warns that those who don't repent of homosexuality will not enter heaven. And you will have seen that the Christian, saved by Jesus, does not continue in that way of life.

This is very hopeful for you because something happens to the Christian that changes him or her. Now he or she is *able* not to indulge in homosexuality. He or she is able to fight against a sinful pattern of same-sex desires and appreciate who they are as a redeemed man or woman able to live in the way of sexual complementarity. This may well mean a heterosexual marriage is possible as God changes desires in that way; it certainly has happened for a good many people in the past. But on the other hand, maybe it won't happen. It surely is not necessary to salvation. But coming to faith does mean embracing biblical manhood for men and womanhood for women even if living a celibate lifestyle for the glory of God. With a new identity comes new behavior.

After seeing that our spiritual identity as Christians lies in what we are *not* anymore, Paul turns to say what we are. We must surely immerse ourselves in his explanation of what has supernaturally happened to the Christian through faith in Christ and by God's grace. See our text once more: 'But you were washed, you were sanctified, you were justified in the name of the Lord Jesus Christ and by the Spirit of our God.' (1 Cor. 6:11) You were washed, Paul says, which means you are washed *now*. You were sanctified which means you are sanctified *now*. You were justified which means you are justified *now*. God has done it to you through grace. What great gospel truths these are!

The Old Man Lurks – but Cannot Control You

Let me apply this specifically to someone who has been actively gay or is experiencing same-sex attraction, but who has repented of this and believed upon Jesus for the forgiveness of their sins. Formerly you were gay, but you have been washed. You have been spiritually cleansed of your guilt of your sin and been born again, clean and new. The power of sin has been broken but the presence is still there. You are the new man, but the old man still lurks.[15] Therefore, having been washed you cannot defile yourself with the dirt of sin anymore. You have died with Jesus in His death and been raised to new life by His Spirit. You must aim at purity because you can. Similarly, formerly you were gay but you have been sanctified. That is to say, you have been separated from that pattern of sexual sin. But it also means that you must be purposeful in your ongoing separation from it.

Finally, formerly you were 'gay,' but now you have been justified. You were unrighteous but now you have been declared righteous. When God convicts us of our sin, we realize our plight and that we have fallen foul of His warnings. Then we look at what we are missing out on and we just long to be in a right relationship with Him – to be legally and officially right with Him. It's like this when you are a child and you have disobeyed your dad. You know you are wrong, you are sorry, and

---

15 See Colossians 3.

you long for things to be right with him again. It's like that with God. You long to be right with Him.

So on the cross Jesus suffers the punishment for the unrighteous gay man or woman and He credits to them His righteous sexually pure life. What grace! Paul puts it like this in 2 Corinthians 5:21, which tells us 'For our sake he made him to be sin who knew no sin, so that in him we might become the righteousness of God.' Peter says it this way in 1 Peter 3:18, where we learn that 'For Christ also suffered once for sins, the righteous for the unrighteous, that he might *bring us to God, being put to death in the flesh but made alive in the spirit ...*'

Now, along with every other sexual sinner, you can be counted righteous in God's eyes as you receive by faith what He has given by grace in Jesus. God, the Father, demands a perfect righteousness in order to be right with Him. God, the Son, provides that for us. So God's justice demands it and His grace provides it. You never grow beyond this truth. It is your rock and your life. It is spiritual gold and the foundation of your faith. Because now you have a perfect legal righteousness before God and all condemnation is removed. God's declaration about you, is 'Justified! Forgiven!'[16] There is no banishment from the kingdom of heaven for you now, only a joyful welcome. When you stand before God on Judgment Day, the ground of your entry into heaven is Christ and His perfect righteous work for you. No matter how holy you become in this life it is always His work that you stand on.

The Christian's Bodily Identity

Not only does Paul tell the Corinthians that they have a new spiritual identity but he also tells them about their bodily identity. This is vital for us to comprehend. God made us as spiritual beings but also *embodied* spiritual beings. What we do with our bodies sexually has great meaning because God made our bodies with divine wisdom and with divine purpose. As my co-author puts it in our book *The Grand Design*: 'When you look at a man, you are supposed to think, God designed that structure – amazing! When you look at a

---

16 We are both forgiven in Christ—through His passive righteousness, His death on the cross—and declared righteous in Christ – through His active righteousness, His perfectly righteous life. For more on these crucial doctrines, see John Murray, *Redemption Accomplished and Applied* (Grand Rapids: Eerdmans, 1955), pp. 117-31.

woman, you are supposed to think, God's own mind created her – incredible!'[17]

With that in mind let's look at 1 Cor. 6:12-20 as we follow the words of that great pastor, the Apostle Paul, and hear his counsel. Without analyzing every word, I shall simply make a few observations about the text in order to inform our understanding of the body. Firstly, note that the body is important because it is for the Lord. But the Lord is also for the body because He made it. '"All things are lawful for me," but not all things are helpful. "All things are lawful for me," but I will not be dominated by anything. "Food is meant for the stomach and the stomach for food" – and God will destroy both one and the other. The body is not meant for sexual immorality, but for the Lord, and the Lord for the body' (1 Cor. 6:12-13).

In other words, your body is for His use. The Lord loves the male and female bodies in the same way a great sculptor loves his works of art, which he carved with his own hands. There is often great misunderstanding in many churches that things of the body are always to be denied. And to be spiritual cannot mean enjoying physical things. This is wrong. The Christian life is spiritual but it is

---

17 Owen Strachan and Gavin Peacock, *The Grand Design: Male and Female He Made Them* (Fearn: Ross-shire, Christian Focus, 2016), p. 100.

earthly in the sense that it is lived out in a physical body that God loves and has designed with desires and needs. But in light of these good purposes the body is not meant for sexual immorality.

Secondly, the body is important because you will one day have a resurrected body. 'And God raised the Lord and will also raise us up by his power' (1 Cor. 6:14). Jesus' resurrection is the beginning of, and prototype for, a general resurrection in resurrected bodies like His. He says it so beautifully in his letter to the Philippians: 'But our citizenship is in heaven, and from it we await a Savior, the Lord Jesus Christ, who will transform our lowly body to be like his glorious body, by the power that enables him even to subject all things to himself' (Phil. 3:20-1). The Christian believer will one day have a body that will never experience the pull or the pain of sin: no same-sex desire anymore.

What good news! The pleasure that this body will have the capacity to feel is described in the Bible as 'joy unspeakable' (1 Pet. 1:8). This means by implication that if you are a Christian you live for something. Paul says in Romans 14:7-8 that 'For not one of us lives for himself, and not one dies for himself; for if we live, we live for the Lord, or if we die, we die for the Lord; therefore whether we live or die, we are the Lord's.' Every fibre of your body is resurrected to live with purpose. That is an amazing thought for anyone in our culture where young men and women are desperately seeking purpose.

Thirdly, the body is important because the Christian is joined to Christ as part of His church, which is His body. 'Do you not know that your bodies are members of Christ? Shall I then take the members of Christ and make them members of a prostitute? Never! Or do you not know that he who is joined to a prostitute becomes one body with her? For, as it is written, "The two will become one flesh." But he who is joined to the Lord becomes one spirit with him.' (1 Cor. 6:15-17). Being joined to Christ is incompatible with all sin and in particular here, sexual sin. In verse 16 he refers to the one flesh union of marriage in Genesis 2:24 and therefore references the fact that marriage between a man and woman is the only place for sexual union. We also know that it has reference to Christ and the church, the Bridegroom and the Bride (Eph. 5:31-2). So the use of the body for sex finds meaning in the greatest truth in the universe. Surely as those who are part of the Bride we cannot defile the Bridegroom or the Bride by indulging in homosexuality. In our mind, we all would reel back from such an idea. So let us live as we ought to think.

Fourthly, the body is important so the Christian will flee sexual immorality and glorify God with his or her body.

Flee from sexual immorality. Every other sin a person commits is outside the body, but the sexually immoral person sins against his own body. Or do you not know that your body is a temple of the Holy Spirit within you, whom you have from God? You are not your own, for you were bought with a price. So glorify God in your body (1 Cor. 6:18-20).

As we are joined to Christ in faith and as the Spirit indwells us, such is our growing repulsion at homosexuality that we do not flirt with that sexual immorality. We flee from it. We get out of its way. Sexual immorality is in a class of its own. It is a sin against one's own body. John Calvin says, 'this sin alone puts a brand of disgrace upon the body … it leaves a stain impressed upon the body, such as is not impressed upon it from other sins.'[18] Great is the mystery of godliness. There is something mysterious about this particular sin and its effects upon us. All other sins are outside but this is committed against the body. It is self-harm. It is taking God's creation—even yourself—and doing something horrible to it. Nonetheless: hope and renewal abound in Jesus Christ.

---

18 Calvin's Commentaries, Vol. XX, *1 Corinthians, II Corinthians* (Baker, 2009), pp. 219-20.

A Story of Transformation

Perhaps some readers wonder if all this doctrine is really workable. Maybe you wonder if this sounds too good to be true. Sure, some people believe what we're laying out, but it's just theoretical. After all, we're not same-sex-attracted, so what relevance do our thoughts have?

The truth is, everyone who stands on God's Word speaks God's own will. This is solid ground, not sinking sand, which man's wisdom represents. It is also true, though, that sound doctrine grounded in the gospel offers people real freedom. Here is one testimony from a man I have counseled extensively; we'll quote it at length as we wrap up this chapter so that you can see that biblical truth really does save and transform sinners like us.[19]

> I first discovered pornography (always gay pornography) at the age of eleven, the year our family got high-speed internet. I was completely unprepared for what I saw, and my teen years were consumed with secret pornography and masturbation. To these destructive habits were added more and more sins, and by the time I started university, I feared both the path I was on and God's judgment on my life. In the middle of

---

19 We requested this testimony, but did not shape or alter it in any way. Though anonymous, it is a real story of deliverance from sin.

a sleepless night I turned to God and confessed all my sins to Him. As a new believer, I had great intentions, but my resolve did not last long as I turned again and again to the same habits. I found I could repent of some sins, but pornography and masturbation had me in a stranglehold. Why did I run to these things over and over again? I could list some reasons – loneliness, boredom, laziness, escape. Ultimately, I didn't know nor believe that life could be better in obedience to God's commands in these areas.

What began as a chance encounter and embedded itself as a habit soon turned into my identity. In the years that followed, I tried to establish myself as sophisticated, educated, talented, and well-socialized, both at work and in the church. I called myself a Christian, but I was proud of my 'struggles' with a sin that was receiving much attention in society (Gay Pride parades became popular and gay marriage was legalized in my teen years). I craved the attention and praise of others. I was a hypocrite, though. At the same time, I lived in a cycle of sexual sin, regret, new resolve, and despair as I attempted to live up to the standard of Christian conduct. I twice joined an online-only counseling program for sexual addicts. I quit both times because it demanded too much of me, and I told myself that the program didn't work. I prayed that God would take away my desires and lead me to a woman that I was attracted to. I didn't realize that God would not only answer my prayers, but also that He would expand my life beyond what I ever thought it could be.

One Sunday, I met a woman named T at church. We became good friends, and I admired her ability to challenge me in areas where I thought I had figured everything out. At our first meeting, I shared with her that I was same-sex-attracted. She accepted that but did not stop there. Months later, I confessed to her that I was also deeply entrenched in pornography and masturbation. T went home and, as she recalled to me later, cried. T prayed for me every day and reminded me of that frequently. I found her prayers and tears uncomfortable, since they presupposed that I was in the wrong. T warned me of the peril of my position and insisted that I find help from a Christian counsellor. I didn't really see the urgency of the situation, but soon reached out to the pastor who had taught in the men's ministry, Gavin.

Gavin directed me to step down from my formal ministry roles. I felt like my world was crashing down, but another pastor reminded me that this was likely God's timing to let this sin go no further, and that it was a time of rebuilding away from the public eye.

During the following two years, I met regularly with Gavin. Gavin assigned me a series of Bible studies, including everything from sex to Christian maturity and the virtue of Christian thankfulness.

During this time, I began to realize how my sin had affected me. I was ineffective in many of my responsibilities because I used them to build up my reputation, not to do good to others or to obey God's will. I learned that I was undisciplined – not just in one area, but in many. I had to learn to wake up on time, eat properly, and exercise. I had to learn to read my Bible daily. I had to learn not to waste time on the internet. I had to learn to have friendships with people that did not struggle with the same things I did and who could be examples of godliness to me.

I also learned how deceptive my own heart was. Creating boundaries became a helpful exercise, and good practice for maturing in other areas of my life. For such a long time, I had acted as if temptation was external to me, but Gavin taught me about the temptations we create for ourselves.

I also learned about God's design for marriage. I thought marriage was about hard self-sacrifice in order to 'get' sex. I didn't realize that biblical marriage was about delight in another. I learned that intimacy was something I had craved, but never had. God used T to show me Christ's love for me. She saw the danger of my position, interceded for me, challenged me, and encouraged me at great personal cost. Her selflessness and kindness attracted me, and God used that to break down the barriers I had put up to intimacy and marriage. In a remarkable act of God's undeserved care to me, we married.

Even more than this, God opened my eyes to see the greatness of salvation in Christ. I knew, at my conversion, that I no longer bore the guilt of past sins. But now I also felt an incredible freedom and courage that came from a clear conscience before God. I have learned about the joy of godly masculinity – the joy of applying all that I am and have in service to Christ and His kingdom. What I lost of my self-made image I have more than gained with the new man He has made me.[20]

Conclusion

We hope this testimony blesses and inspires you, whatever your background, whatever your current experience. As our friend discovered, Christ is worth everything. Though we fall into sin of many kinds, including the sin of homosexuality, Christ makes all things new. This conviction seems to be waning in focus among the professing church today; people wonder if conversion really changes, really delivers, really transforms. To be sure we must all battle the flesh daily; there is no perfect believer in this life. Nonetheless as the true story above shows in abundance, God makes all things new through His Word and His Spirit.

He has not stopped doing so.

---

20 For a similarly powerful testimony from a woman, see Emily Thomes, 'My Story,' accessible at http://emilythomes.com/my-story. Last accessed January 2020.

3. THE FAITHFUL FIGHT AGAINST SEXUAL SIN

━━━━━

Thus far we have covered both the 'bad news' and the 'good news' of our condition. We have learned that every sinner is in a terrible state before the Lord. We have seen that homosexuality is an abomination and an offense to God. Yet we have studied in depth the lengths to which God Himself has gone to rescue sinners from sin, Satan, death, and hell. We have covered at length the glorious gospel of the Bible. We have seen that every sinner is infinitely lost, but that God has given the infinitely great gift of His only Son to redeem us. In a world that feels endlessly paranoid and relentlessly hopeless, we have declared that there is no hope like this.

Now, in this chapter, we build off of the previous discussion. We are going to assume all that we just traced. In other words, the application we give here is directly connected to the power of the gospel. We are not commending a 'get yourself sorted out' exercise here. We do not want you to confuse what follows with 'self-help,' for example. This is not 'self-help' – not even close. This is 'salvation help.' The following commitments and practices go hand in hand with the gospel. As you believe the truth, the truth washes over you, and activates your will. You begin to see areas that need spiritual work. You recognize the necessity of personal change. But all this effort—and it is real effort you must put in here—is motivated by a great and glorious vision of a saving and transforming God.

These matters will apply most directly to those battling same-sex attraction. But they are also applicable to many Christians as we shall see. Our goal here is not to zap a certain group of sinners; our goal here is to show in practical form what it looks like to leave behind the snare of homosexuality. Truly, this is not inconsequential stuff. This is what it looks like—going back to Chapter 1—to flee Sodom, to run away from same-sex sin as fast as you can, always while looking ahead to the One who has made a way of escape: Christ Jesus. Toward that end, here are six practical steps to take in order to leave homosexuality behind.

First Step: Deal with Your Past

Before we launch into the future, it is good to think hard about our history. We want to think hard about why we have sinned against God. This is true for us all. We want to think hard about same-sex attraction. Are there factors in our background that helped feed this sin? Is there brokenness we can identify that has led us to think that homosexuality is the answer? Did homosexuality become our identity in an 'out and proud' way, or was it a hidden identity that we covered with shame? We need to ask these and many other questions of this kind.

In doing so, we are emulating the Psalmist. Psalm 139 features this outcry: 'Search me, O God, and know my heart! Try me and know my thoughts! And see if there be any grievous way in me, and lead me in the way everlasting!' (Ps. 139:23-4). This is a present reality, of course. But it applies as well to our whole experience of sin. Crying out for God to 'search' us means that we are inviting the Spirit to turn us inside out. We are asking God to perform a spiritual X-ray on our soul and body. We are not hiding anything from Him. In truth, we can't hide anything from Him, but the point is plain: we do not *want* to hide from Him. Perhaps we did. Perhaps the sin of homosexuality (like many others) brought us great shame. Perhaps we were thankful in a dark way that no human person knew our thoughts. But now, through conversion, we know that God does know our thoughts. He knows our heart. We do not want to run from Him. We invite Him to search us.

It will likely be best that we do this ourselves but also with the help of wise counselors in the faith. We'll say more in our sixth application about the church, but here we will simply note that 'searching' of this kind may be painful. It may dredge up feelings of shame and guilt. Many of us are accustomed to hiding, and are skilled at it. We run from 'searching,' thinking that doing so preserves and helps us. But the opposite is true. In running from self-examination at worst and God-examination at best, we are running from the truth. We are avoiding confrontation with ourselves. We are ensuring that the visceral battle for our health endures without resolution.

So we stop running. We reckon with our past. It is good that we peel back the layers of days gone by with a godly leader or friend. If our life experience is akin to a house with many rooms, there are rooms that will be difficult to enter alone. No person's experience is another person's. Yet we will note that some people will have to deal with past abuse, either abuse done to them or abuse committed. Some will find sin done to them in the past, sin they did not ask for, sin they hated but were powerless to escape. Some will see a fractured relationship with a father or mother, or an over-reliance on one parent.

Some will see moments of quiet curiosity that came seemingly from nowhere but blossomed into actions later on in life. Some will see confusion, real confusion, about their identity and desires; their struggle with homosexuality was a push-and-pull reality, sometimes positive in their past perspective, sometimes negative. Some will see intentional rebellion, raw and powerful, against biblical truth and creational design. Their past includes advocacy for the homosexual cause, anger toward those who opposed it, and celebration of pagan behavior.

There is no exact 'blueprint' for people who have fallen into homosexuality in past days. The Bible, frankly, does not feature any lengthy section about the psychology of same-sex attraction and the various experiences of those who have dealt with it. The Bible provides us with just what we need: it tells us the truth about God's design. It tells us the truth about straying from this design. It tells us how we may return to God's design. I think we can say with confidence that the Bible comprehends numerous elements in a person's background that relate to this sin (and any other). Our doctrine of depravity is not small; it is big.

This means that we can account for long, spiraling tales of compromise, evil, and personal destruction. There are and will be 'grievous way[s]' in us, and some of those terrible ways have been cut long before the present moment (Ps. 139:24).

But we are not taken aback by this; we shouldn't be. We shouldn't be surprised as Christians by a person having a sinful past. All of us do in some form. All of us know within us the bitter yet spicy taste of temptation toward ungodly things. Even more piercingly, we all must fight against perversity *now*, as believers; we all must confess our sin of mind and heart *today*, recognizing that even in our Christian walk we sometimes entertain terrible things in our inner man, and sometimes do and say and want terrible things.

Second Step: Reject a Homosexual Identity

As we have just examined, we are tempted to believe that our past is our present, and is our future. We may not consciously trace this thinking back to Satan himself, but it does. Satan desperately wants us to deny the gospel truth that there is an 'old man' and there is a 'new man' (see Rom. 6:6). Satan works very hard to get us to believe that there is only the 'old man.' He gives great energy to try to induce Christians (and those considering the claims of Christ) to think that there is no such thing as conversion, there is no growth in godliness, there is no new identity in Jesus. We are who we were, nothing more. Put more personally, I am who I was.

But as we saw in Chapter 2, this is all lies. This is hell itself speaking in our ear. It is anti-gospel to say and believe that the 'old man' is the 'new man.' Yes, we are the same person; we have the same background, the same general body, the same collection of experiences. But as Gavin spelled out, we have become new. This is the miracle of Christianity, isn't it? Those ruined and wracked and destroyed by sin may shed their sinful identity. Like a moth turning into a butterfly, they may become new in and through Christ. Their past does not define them. We can put it more strongly: our past cannot define us. The blood of Christ has washed us. The grace of God has saved us. The verdict of 'justified' has been given to us. We have a past, but the past is not where we stay. The past is not what defines us. Christ is. We cannot stress this strongly enough.

All this informs our understanding of our past in a deeper and richer way. It may seem like we were 'born this way'; or it may be that we realized our patterns of attraction developed toward the same sex over time. Whether our ungodliness is lifelong or has only debuted in recent days, our response to it is the same: we kill that sin. We never own it as a positive or neutral part of our life. We try to identify where it is influencing us and why (as much as we can), but we always come back to the biblical call to 'put off' the old man and 'put on' the new (Col. 3:1-11).

This point matters hugely for our engagement of our culture in 2020. Calling our homosexual identity an 'orientation' does not change anything about the Bible's witness on this count. We hear this language used today in secular settings, and we are told that our 'orientation' is just the way we are, not anything that should occasion change or transformation or separation. But this secular thinking does not countermand the Bible. As we have studied, homosexuality is in no way neutral in the biblical account. It is not neutral in terms of behavior; it surely is not neutral in terms of our self-understanding. Same-sex 'orientation' is akin to same-sex identity. We can no more have a same-sex 'orientation' as a Christian than we can find our identity in anything unrighteous. You might have a natural pull to something, that's true. The question before us is whether what we are naturally drawn to is God-glorifying or God-dishonoring.[1]

---

1   For sound words on the use of 'orientation' language regarding homosexuality, see Burk and Lambert, *Transforming Homosexuality*, pp. 19-38. Burk and Lambert help us see that even if we allow for a concept like 'orientation' as an enduring pattern of attraction, this in no way enfranchises the thinking behind unbiblical 'orientation' that frames it as a neutral or positive state.

Do old temptations still pull at us? Yes, we shall cover that in what follows. But those temptations—though real—do not and cannot shape our identity. God has given us a new name, a new identity, a new present, and a new future. We are not who we were. We are not who Satan wants us to believe we are. So, we say with love and compassion: reject your past identity. Preach this truth to yourself: I am a new creation in Christ. I am born again. I am a Christian. I am washed, waiting, and justified. Sin does not define me. Homosexuality *cannot* define me, strong as its pull once was, much as I may still need to fight temptation. Only Christ can and does shape my identity.

Some may find this struggle lessen quickly after conversion. Some may find it receding over time. Some may have to fight this battle every day they live. There is no one-size-fits-all experience on this count. But whatever your struggle relative to your identity, whether it is clean or combative over the long haul, do not forget that Christ is not only a part of our life; He *is* our life (Col. 3:4).

Third Step: Fight Homosexual Thoughts and Desires and Forsake Homosexual Actions

The call of Christ is a call to forsake sin. There is no true conversion in the name of Jesus that is not accompanied by a whole-soul turning from sin. When we turn *to* Christ, we turn *from* sin. This is not true for one kind of sinner who has one particular battle with the flesh. This is true of us all. Everyone who loves Jesus hates their depravity. Everyone who hates their depravity fights it tooth and nail.

The first dimension of this battle centers in our identity. We covered that above. But the battle has a second dimension. Once we know our identity, we are freed and able to break with sinful thoughts. Think of Romans 12:1-2 on this matter:

> *I appeal to you therefore, brothers, by the mercies of God, to present your bodies as a living sacrifice, holy and acceptable to God, which is your spiritual worship. Do not be conformed to this world, but be transformed by the renewal of your mind, that by testing you may discern what is the will of God, what is good and acceptable and perfect.*

God is not after either heart or mind, Paul teaches here. God wants whole-person transformation. How does this happen? It happens as our mind is renewed. Prior to our conversion, in different ways we were *thoroughly* conformed to this world. Now, by the power of Christ in us —'by the mercies of God'—we conform our mind to 'what is good and acceptable and perfect.' This is the will of God. Whatever is good to think about is God's will for us to think about; whatever is acceptable to God is God's will for us to think about; whatever is excellent, and lovely, and admirable is God's will for us to think about.

In practical terms, when we think wrong thoughts, we should confess them to God, repent of them, and ask Him for power over the flesh. This in turn helps us fight the battle for our desires, for what the mind is fixed upon, the heart will want. If the mind is fixed upon Christ, in general the heart will want Christ. If the mind is fixed upon sin, the heart will want sin. No Christian gets this just right, alas; we all must repent regularly of allowing our mind, and thus our heart, to be drawn away by our own wrong thoughts and lustful passions (see James 1:13-15). Though this happens, we nonetheless keep fighting for holiness. We pray according to Philippians 2:13 and know that 'it is God who works in you' to grow us in righteousness. As this is gloriously true, we also ask God 'to will and to work for his good pleasure.' In other words, we ask God to refocus our mind on Christ, and we ask God to give us a fresh desire to obey Him.

We can put this more simply. On the subject of homosexuality (and like it every battle with the flesh), we should fight wrong thoughts, and we should fight wrong desires. When we think things that are not true, believing even for a flicker that homosexuality is not wrong, we should repent of this thought and counter this idea with the truth of God's Word. When we feel a momentary burst of lust for someone of the same sex, we should repent of this desire and pray for God to help us 'will and work for his good pleasure' (Phil. 2:13 again).

We have covered this in Book One but will repeat it here: a thought or desire is not wrong because you feel it especially strongly or for a long time. A thought or desire is wrong when it is focused on something ungodly. To think untrue things about homosexuality for even an instant calls for repentance. To have even a quick flash of same-sex attraction toward someone calls for repentance. Our thinking and desiring is not wrong only when we entertain sin in some form for ten seconds, for example. There is no 'ten second rule' to be found in the Bible. Thinking and desiring is wrong when it is focused on sinful ends and sinful things.

If you share this with a fellow sinner (of any kind), they may say something like 'But that's an impossible standard!' They may go on to say, 'I'll end up depressed following that sort of theology, because I'll need to repent a lot.' This is exactly the point! We do need to repent. This is not something we do sometimes, on even days of the week. This is every day. This is, further, how we grow. We train our spiritual muscles to get stronger. We take every thought captive as we discipline our minds. We rule over once unruly bodies. Is this a high standard? Yes. It is the very standard of God. Yet we rest assured that the grace of God is sufficient for us. God will help us grow, progressively and over the long haul of our lives, in conformity to His holiness.

This mental transformation prompts a bodily transformation. We cease to present our bodies as servants of Satan. Instead, we present our bodies as 'living sacrifices' to God. As our mind is cleansed, so our body is cleansed. This has major importance for the sin of homosexuality, which is a sin—as we have seen—against God's design, against the body, against 'nature' (Rom. 1:26). This leads into the third dimension to our great war against evil: our forsaking of sinful actions.

The gift of divine love always comes with a hammer. You do not get saved and sit in your room, thinking precious thoughts unto God. You get saved and you go smash your idols. You go to war on the flesh. You do violence to your sin (see Paul's attitude in 1 Cor. 9:26-7). This means in practical terms for our study that those saved by grace make a clean break with homosexual actions. If there are places you went to gratify the flesh, you stop going to them. If there are websites you visited with lustful intent, you stop visiting them. If your smartphone is a perpetual temptation to you, you might well downgrade to a 'dumb phone.' Whatever your precise circumstances, the point is plain: anything needed to forsake sin, we do.

Fourth Step: Return to Biblical Manhood and Womanhood

We commonly hear today in evangelical circles that 'holiness is not straightness.' In other words, when we get saved, God isn't calling us to get married, necessarily. Further, we might get saved and never lose a general homosexual orientation. We can be homosexual in terms of our broader experience but still trust Christ as Savior.

We are thankful for anyone who loves the gospel of grace. Further, we are thankful when we hear someone confess that they have left homosexual relationships and actions behind. But the 'holiness is not straightness' line simply does not go far enough. Though undoubtedly stated with good intentions, it does not do full justice to the lordship of Jesus Christ in every believer's life. As we saw in Chapter 2, Paul identified both the active and passive partner in a homosexual relationship. He said that these— along with numerous other kinds of rebellious sinner—would not 'inherit the kingdom of God' (1 Cor. 6:10). What a jolt of a statement that is.

We address what biblical manhood and biblical womanhood look like in greater detail in Book Three of this trilogy. Our remarks on this issue can only be brief here. For now, it is enough to note that the gospel enables we who are the 'new creation' (2 Cor. 5:17) to embrace creation, God's design. We may get married or not following our conversion; some former homosexuals will, and some will not. Some will find a desire for marriage, including the instinct for godly sexual union with a spouse of the opposite sex, develop in them. Some will not. Marriage is honorable and a spouse is a good gift of God. In Christ, anything is possible.

Yet we must note carefully here that getting married does not make us a godly man or a godly woman. The former homosexual person is called to biblical manhood or womanhood the exact same way any Christian is called to own their God-given sex and roles in life. Men need to be trained to be a leader, protector, and provider, whether for themselves alone or for a family. Women need to be trained to receive and honor male leadership, nurture life, and practice godly domesticity, whether for themselves alone or for a family. The sexes alike need to know, esteem, and embrace God's creational design.

Through the gospel, we see that we enjoy complementary unity, polarity, and reciprocity with all believers. Whether complementary interest develops in adolescence and blossoms into complementary desire for marriage in adulthood, every born-again person is a man or a woman according to their birth sex. Through salvation, they come to treasure their own sex, they relate rightly as a brother or sister to the same sex, and they value the opposite sex as that made for the full glory of God. They cling to no attraction to the same sex, they retain no trace of their former identity, and they understand that any godly sexual desire is oriented to the covenant of marriage.

It is not that the redeemed man or woman is in some sort of neutral state; they are a man or a woman, made even in a broader non-marital way to image God's glory in complementary relationship with the opposite sex. It is not that every man is the covenantal head of every woman, as one outworking of this truth; it is that godly men see themselves as leaders, protectors, and providers, and godly women receive and honor this truth. Men honor and support women in their God-made identity; women honor and support men in their God-made identity. The sexes together work to celebrate and live out God's good design in the church.

There will be practical effects to this reorientation to God's design. Men will need discipleship in biblical manhood. There is no exact psychological method we have in mind here; rather, in terms roughly akin to familial instruction, mature men need to help new converts leave behind effeminacy, whether of tone, demeanor, voice, presentation, dress (to name just a few areas of growth). Women will need discipleship to reject 'manly womanhood,' whether in manner, dress, demeanor, presentation, voice (to name just a few areas of growth). Men who embrace biblical manhood from a homosexual background will not all look or act the same, nor will the same be true for redeemed women. Nonetheless, godly men and women will seek to love and live according to God's distinctive design for the sexes (see 1 Cor. 11, for example).[2]

If this sounds odd, we should think once more of Paul's teaching to the Corinthian church. Corinthian men saved out of a homosexual life-style could not act or identify as they once did. They were made new. They were called out of pagan identity and behavior, and called into Christian identity and behavior.[3] The Bible has

---

2   As we have pointed out, this discipleship is much closer to familial instruction (father to son, mother to daughter) than it is to a secular psychotherapeutic method dependent on secular ideas, however well-intentioned.

3   Training here involves a way-of-life grounded in truth. It is less about techniques and secular methods and more about holistic instruction and communication of biblical wisdom.

much to say about being a godly man or a godly woman; the biblical authors clearly understood that conversion means owning God's design and living it out. In truth, it is not that we are merely 'returning' to God's design through salvation. We are becoming who we were meant to be.

'Straightness' is not holiness, it turns out. But embracing biblical manhood *is* holiness. Embracing biblical womanhood *is* holiness. This is true if you get married; this is true if you remain single all your days. Growing as a man or woman of God is not a burden or an option, it turns out. It is a delight, a privileged calling, the experience of God's goodness for the men and women He made for His glory.

Fifth Step: Embrace the Goodness of the Local Church

The Christian life is not meant to be an isolated struggle against the flesh. Sometimes it may feel that way, but God has a better way for us: membership in a local church. Joining and serving a church will not magically cure all the troubles you face. It will, however, ensure that you have help and support and familial care as you make your way to glory.

If you are leaving homosexuality behind, you will find in the church several strengthening aids. First, you will receive teaching about the Christian life. It won't be up to you to figure everything out as a believer. You'll learn much from the Bible about what faith looks like in a fallen world. As you sit under the Word, God will renew your mind, refocus your heart, and feed your soul. As we discussed earlier, expository preaching executes a dual mission: it de-conforms you from the world, and conforms you to the Word (Rom. 12:1-2). We all need this. God knew that we needed the ministry of the Word so much—so very much—that He instituted it weekly.

You will also find examples, counselors, and a family. There is no one in the church who can zap your problems and make them all vanish on the spot. But there are godly men and women who, like you, are committed to battling their sins for the rest of their lives. These are believers, and they are zeroed in on holiness. They hate their sin and they love Jesus Christ. They will encourage you in your walk with God; they will give you solid counsel in tough moments; they will check in on you and help you cross the line. They are part of the 'household' of God as you are, and they will provide encouragement and blessing to you as you walk with Christ through the ups and downs of life (Eph. 2:19).[4]

---

4   The Christian family—the local church based on the universal church—does not replace the natural family. The New Testament does nothing to de-prioritize the natural family, but rather brings families and singles together in fellowship.

They will give you an example, furthermore, of following Christ through trials. We all need this, for we all face hardships of various kinds. In trusting Christ, we see in the church, we have all embraced the way of the cross. No one is untouched by suffering. Seeing others do this day by difficult day—and doing so with joy in their spirit—will help us when we feel as if our burden is too great. Thankfully, we are not alone, and we are not abandoned to our difficulties. Thanks to the Father's will (Eph. 1:1-14), we have Christ, we have the Spirit, and we have the fellowship of the saints.[5]

In the church, you will also be able to re-form your friendships. Part of what is needed in leaving sin behind, including homosexual sin, are healthy and rightly-oriented friendships.[6] There may be some awkwardness in navigating the world of the church; even a small congregation has its little social ecosystem. But the local church helps Christians of every kind leave worldly friendship behind, friendship that is structured along mutual pursuit

---

5   Thanks be to God for the holy Trinity, the first family. The three persons work in perfect harmony to save us and bring us home.

6   We need to be clear that identifying as 'gay' does not make you better able to enjoy same-sex friendship. Homosexual inclinations corrupt true friendship, sadly. It is only when we reject homosexuality that we will be able to best experience friendship as God intends.

of worldly pleasure, personal gain, social climbing, greater reputation, and other ungodly ends. In the church, people may well have little in common but faith in Jesus Christ. This can be challenging, but it can also be freeing. You are liberated from connecting only to your 'tribe,' and are gloriously unburdened to get to know Christians of many ages, backgrounds, and classes.

What a blessing the church is to us needy people. Joining a church, and then figuring out a way to serve and strengthen that church, will bring hope and meaning and joy to your heart. The church, after all, is the 'pillar and buttress' of the truth (1 Tim. 3:15). It backs up and reinforces and solidifies in our minds what the Word itself teaches. How we need this, all of us! We were not made to walk the narrow way alone. We need the Lord, and we need the fellowship of the church.

Sixth Step: Savor Christ Continually

Our final word is a simple one. In all our trials, we must look to Christ, the author and finisher of our faith. He is the center of our faith, not us. He gets all the glory, not us. He gives us all the grace we need, not us. He is our joy and treasure, not sin. He has given us all His righteousness; He has taken all our sin (Rom. 5). Jesus is not only the gateway to the Christian life; Jesus *is* the Christian life.

We no longer find our identity in anyone but Jesus. Jesus has overwhelmed us, and conquered us, and won us back. Remember Colossians 3:4, where Christ is said to be *our life*. If you know Jesus, He is your identity; He is your reputation; He is your hope; He is your redeemer; He is your all in all; He is your life itself. This constellation of biblical truths is not depressing to the truly-saved individual. It is freeing in extremity. We are no longer captive to the prison of our past, our pride, our thanklessness, our sin. We are liberated.

These realities will bear you up amidst the struggles and failings of everyday existence. Truth and doctrine is your greatest weapon against the enemy and against yourself. You must daily preach Christ to yourself; you must daily set your eyes upon Him, and choose the joy of knowing Him over the temporal 'pleasure' of indulging the flesh. We do this best when we soak up the Word daily and pray in a focused way to the Lord. Savoring Christ is not a contractual commitment on paper; it is a living exercise, and daily devotions—generally speaking—help us do it in a rich and focused way.

Conclusion

In the end, it turns out that the battle against homosexuality is not really about sex in any form. It's about Christ. Will we bow to Him? Will we worship Him all our days? Or will we follow our own heart? Will we worship ourselves and fellow creatures? The stakes are very high on this count. They are eternal. Following anything but the Word of God leads to eternal damnation. This reality leads Christians to genuine fear and compassion for those drawn to homosexuality who resist repentance and faith in the name of Christ. We do not speak the truth, the whole biblical truth, out of hatred for sinners. We speak the truth out of love, praying that fellow lost people will trust Christ.

Now is the time to flee Sodom. Now is the time to run to the hills. Look ahead as you run, and you will see one who has gone ahead. It is Christ Jesus. The world is on fire, and opportunities to lose your soul for eternity abound. Many around you make just this choice. They pursue sin and give approval to those who do so. Do not follow them. Look ahead, and keep your eyes lasered in on Jesus. He has made a way for you out of Sodom. He has bought back sinners from the dead.

FREQUENTLY ASKED QUESTIONS

What Does the Bible Teach About Homosexuality?

In this section of the book, we address questions people frequently raise surrounding the issue of homosexuality. Our aim here is not to give lengthy and exhaustive answers to these good queries, but is instead to build off of the content of this book and give short, readable, practical guidance on these subjects. We cite Scripture as our authority and guide, but in some answers below we give biblically-shaped wisdom where there are gray areas.

1. I am fifteen and feel consistently attracted to the same sex. Am I gay?

It is better to say that you experience same-sex desires on a regular basis. But this doesn't mean you are gay. To say you are gay is to embrace the identity. You could also just be experiencing part of what is known as puberty. The body is changing rapidly; hormones are coursing through your veins as they kick in and that can make you feel all sorts of strange things. You may simply be experiencing admiration and affection for another of the same sex, which is quite common amongst teenagers but doesn't mean you are gay. If you are not a Christian we encourage you to come to Jesus and embrace Him as your Lord and Savior. This is what you need first – to find your identity in Jesus. The rest flows from there as we have covered in our book. If you are a Christian then once you've decided whether these are sexual desires or simply admiration and affection, you can repent where necessary and trust the Lord to reorder you towards what we have described as complementary unity, polarity, and reciprocity.

2. Can we train our children not to be gay?

Fathers and mothers are vital in modeling and training their children in the way they should go. This is why we need distinctly complementarian marriages where the sexes are distinct and defined even as they are presented as equally valuable. With these things noted, children may face same-sex attraction (SSA) from an early age, or this may develop in them as time goes on, or they may consciously choose it at some point. In our homes, we must teach and model the truth, lovingly guiding our children to God's will, lovingly—and clearly—steering them away from all that is unrighteous. Teaching about the sinfulness of homosexuality is not a knee-jerk matter, then; it should be part of a whole-life education in the beauty of manhood, womanhood, marriage, and the family.

We cannot at the end of the day save or make obedient our children. Fathers must lead their families well, caring for members spiritually (see 1 Tim. 3:1-7 on the home of the elder). Yet they must not exasperate their children by brow-beating them into holiness (see Eph. 6, Col. 3). Fathers and mothers must pray regularly for their children, asking the Lord to apply the continual teaching of their Christian home to the heart of their child such that the little ones under their care trust Christ at a young age and repent in the name of Christ.

3. My child is being taught at school that gay is okay. What should I do?

We think you have freedom on this count, though you must think very carefully about this matter, and not take it lightly. You can remove your child from this school (and not put your children in such schools). If you do keep them in the school, you need to make sure that you are teaching them very clearly from the Scripture about the sinfulness of homosexuality. Do note that keeping them in the school means not merely that they hear a few minutes of pedagogy on unholy sexuality, but that they are likely to be in an environment that supports and promotes this worldview in diverse ways. We cannot save our children, and the Bible does not tell us precisely how to educate our kids. But we have responsibility before the Lord of protecting our kids, helping them, shielding them from evil in appropriate forms, and pointing them to Christ.

It is surely true—as some Christians will note—that we should not pretend that the world is unfallen. It is very difficult to raise children in fallen places, especially when sin is celebrated, as it now is in many places in the West. Doing so takes much prayer, thought, marital togetherness, and involvement in a strong local church that disciples children in the truth. We do not think there is only one way to educate children, but we do think that our context requires very honest thinking about how to best shepherd and protect our children in these times. It is no bad thing in the least to home-school children, have them in classical or Christian schools, or use other such options as desired. Part of what is needed here, in closing, is an assessment of one's children – are they drawn to sin? Do they seem resistant to it? How is the world affecting them?

4. Should I let my child play at the house of his friend who has two mums?

This is not clearly answered in Scripture. We would note that Christian fathers and mothers must take great care to protect their children and shepherd them. There is no imperative in Scripture regarding one's children being exposed to ungodliness. Instead, the emphasis in the Bible is on training one's children in righteousness. While we should seek to love all people and be a witness to them, it is hard for us to imagine Israelite children playing with Canaanite children. It is true that the New Testament has a more evangelistic focus, but again, our children are not missionaries. Are we training them to share the gospel and live a sold-out life for Christ? Yes, ideally. But we must do this with great care, and without putting any pressure on them to be an evangelist at age eight. The Bible warns us about drawing near to ungodly influences, even as it commends spending time with the wise (see Ps. 1; Prov. 13:20). We do well to structure our kids' relationships along these lines.

5. How should we handle a fifteen year old who comes out as gay and wants to date someone of the same sex?

We refer you to our answer to the first question for a start. We also presume you have taught them the gospel and the biblical worldview on sexuality and they have clearly rejected it. With that said we advise two further steps. Firstly, you assume your parental responsibility and authority. You make the household rules and as Christians these rules are based on biblical guidelines. Secondly, explain that you wouldn't let the child date anyone at this stage of life. It is not wise. Tell them you want them to be open with you about their feelings and that they can tell you anything and you will still love them even if you don't always approve of their views.

To summarize we advise a display of loving authority and empathetic communication. Underpin this with fervent prayer for your child.

6. Should you attend a 'gay wedding'?

We would say no because attending a gay wedding is to affirm its moral validity. The minister/pastor will traditionally ask the congregation if anyone knows just cause why the two should not be married. To remain silent at that point means to agree with the union. We cannot celebrate what is clearly against God's design and desire and violates His law. By attending we would be publicly affirming something as marriage that is not marriage and that cannot be.

If we did turn down such an invitation, we would encourage respectful and gracious conversation with the participants. In other words, we believe Christians have an opportunity in such moments to articulate the gospel and biblical worldview in a kind yet convictional form.

7. If your son or daughter marries someone of the same sex, how do you continue to love him or her?

Whilst we would not have attended the so-called wedding, we would invite them over and love them both. We would have them over to dinner and partake as much as Christian conscience will allow. This means that they would not be allowed to sleep together in our own homes. In this way we would love the child and their partner and treat them with the dignity all image-bearers deserve. But we would honor God first. That is the best witness to them as well as another way we can love our child.

8. How do you approach a gay couple that enters your church building?

Just the way you would welcome anyone else. Welcome them warmly and pray they are saved by the gospel. Follow up with them as you would with any newcomer. Pray for them and think strategically about how you will answer their questions when they come. We are not trying in any way to keep unbelievers of any kind from attending our services; while we have a responsibility to shepherd the congregation, we very much want lost people of every background to hear the preached Word, experience the welcoming of the church, and ultimately come to faith in Christ. But none of this witness involves endorsing or approving of any sin pattern or ungodly lifestyle.

9. I am a Christian gym owner. I hold couples classes and a gay couple want to participate? What's the Christian response?

This might pose a problem for you. To refuse them when you've openly advertised couples (or even married couples) classes, might mean you will have to accept their participation. Here is the point. Nowadays Christian businesses need to think very carefully and we would suggest taking Christian legal counsel with regards to how business owners word things on websites and advertising literature and where they stand legally in view of potential LGBT pressures.

10. Should a celibate Christian man who experiences same-sex attraction be allowed to serve in leadership in the local church?

There is debate among godly theologians and pastors over whether single men can be elders.

The normative expectation of God, at the very least, is that elders be married and raise children, and thrive in these callings (1 Tim. 3:1-7; Titus 1:5-9). We do not want to dismiss these elements of elderly qualification lightly.

Admittedly there is real gray area here. Let us leave aside the question of eldership. Much depends on the level of struggle a man faces. Men who are experiencing real defeat in the area of SSA should not lead and teach in the church, just as married men who are slipping into sin with pornography or other women must not lead and teach in the church. While admitting there is some need for clarity on this count, we want to lay the stress where the Bible does: on consistent godliness. The Scripture gives us a high standard for leadership. It calls into the eldership—specifically—men who excel as husbands, fathers, and spiritual leaders. Whatever hard questions we face, we want to uphold this standard.

11. How should a Christian who still experiences same-sex attraction deal with friendships of the same sex?

Wisely and hopefully! Keep a short account of sin and be watchful over yourself. Avoid one-to-one situations, which might inflame desire. Group friendships are advisable. But the church can provide a family environment for holy same-sex friendships – that gives us hope for healthy companionship. We can have same-sex friendship as long as we understand these friendships biblically and not as a replacement for marriage (or to be held in higher esteem than marriage).

We also want to be quite careful about living together, making covenantal commitments to one another that are not marital but are more than normal, and vacationing together in potentially compromising circumstances. Such actions may feel right, but we want to cleave to wisdom. This is true through the Christian life. It is ideal to have healthy same-sex friendships under the care and account-ability of the local church, but to be very cautious about taking drastic steps beyond this. We note these things because we are all called to be watch-ful, to take our sin seriously, and to not think that we are strong in our own strength – for we are not.

12. If a homosexual person has been saved, should they cut all ties with the gay community or should they seek to evangelize it?

Because of the nature of the sin one would need to have a high level of mastery over one's desires and have a firm grasp of their identity in Christ and sense of community in the church before entering into gay-community evangelism. At the same time we wouldn't say it is a wrong aim. And naturally, if you were formerly homosexual, there will be a desire to see some snatched from the fire as you were. It would simply need to be approached very wisely. Much depends here on one's level of maturity, and one's ability to navigate potentially tempting situations. As we have said repeatedly, accountability and connection to the church—ideally to godly members or elders—is necessary and good.

13. If I want to find a church that preaches and teaches the doctrine this book unfolds, how can I find one?

We hope and pray this happens as a result of this little book. God loves the local church, and calls us to join one in membership (see Matthew 18; 1 Corinthians 5; Hebrews 10:25). We would encourage you to find a church that clearly and happily affirms the following: the Chicago Statement on Biblical Inerrancy, the Danvers Statement on Biblical Manhood and Womanhood, and the Nashville Statement on Biblical Sexuality.

14. If we tell the truth about homosexual sin, won't lost people tune us out, causing us to lose our witness?

There is no tension between telling the truth and loving fellow sinners. It is loving, in fact, to tell the truth. Our proclamation of God's teaching, then, does not get in the way of Christian witness. Christian proclamation is Christian witness. We need to supplement our speech with the fruits of the Spirit, to be sure. We cannot think that we should only speak up and do no more. We are called to be 'light,' after all, to shimmer with life and love and the beauty of holiness (Matt. 5:17-20). But do not be mistaken: the natural man does not receive the things of God (1 Cor. 2:14). People may well disagree with, dislike, and even despise us for telling the truth about homosexuality. They could even go so far as to persecute us, as happened with Christ, as happened with His apostles, as has happened to countless Christians over the centuries.

Come what may, we must not lose sight of the fact that we are called to speak the truth in love. There is no new mission for Christians today; there is no new way for the church to proclaim God's Word. Pastors must lead out in this great calling; if our pulpits are mighty in the Scriptures, our people will be mighty in the Scriptures.[1] It is true that our own context may have its own sinful predilections, but we

---

1   To better understand how every pastor is called to be a theologian, see Kevin J. Vanhoozer and Owen Strachan, *The Pastor as Public Theologian: Reclaiming a Lost Vision* (Grand Rapids: Baker Academic, 2015).

must not overdo 'contextual' witness. While always taking stock of where we are, we must remember that every place and every people has a truly desperate need for God, His gospel, and His Word. This is what the church gathered is in business to provide; this is what the church scattered strives to declare.

In the end, we will not be measured by results in themselves. We will be measured in divine terms by faithfulness to the Word of God, not any earthly metric of popularity, fame, or success.

15. You've given practical counsel in Chapter 2 of this book, but as a counselor or discipler in the church I want a fuller 'method' by which to walk people through gospel transformation and the everyday fight for faith. Any suggestions?

This book is a partnership; the method below is one we have worked out together based on sound biblical doctrine, and that Gavin in particular has identified and applied in his pastoral work with numerous men and women. We call it the 'Delineation of Desire' approach.

1. **Discern** if the person is a Christian or not. This makes a huge difference. If they are Christian they need discipleship and counseling. If they are not they need evangelism and conversion. The first

thing anyone needs is Christ. If they are saved they then, as a new creation, have the spiritual ability to go on being transformed by the renewal of their mind (Rom. 12:1-2).

2. **Draw** the person out. Gather information about their background and current life situation. This shows that when you speak the truth you love them as a person made in the image of God and don't regard them simply as a project (Eph. 4:25). It is also valuable in seeing what outside influences there have been upon their sin, and if there are certain trigger situations where their sin manifests itself regularly.

3. **Detail** the significance of the gospel and what union with Christ means. If not a Christian, call them to faith in Christ. If they are a Christian, remind them that God could never love them less or more than He does in that moment, that their sins are forgiven and there is no legal guilt for them anymore. And that they have both the freedom and the power to overcome sin and put it to death. But also remind them that they must do this.

4. **Delineate** the design. As we have discussed, take people to the framework of biblical sexuality. Apply their situation to the good and wise design of God, and show them how faith in Christ affirms divine creation for all who are a new creation in Christ.

5. **Detect** the flesh. This flows from point two. Knowing the person and their story helps detect what might be underlying sins beneath the sin. (Sometimes sins cluster together, and sometimes they come on their own, even as all sin is idolatry.) In light of the previous point and a clear under-standing of sin, identify what drives their specific sin patterns: is it desire to be worshiped, fear of man, envy, vengeance, power that underpins the sin they manifest?

6. **Destroy** the sin. Once the person has identified sins beneath sin they are in a position to kill sin at root. Realizing their union with Christ they can name the sin(s) and turn from them. This repent-ance must happen at impulse level.

7. **Draw** near to Christ. Put on Christ – put on the new self (Col. 3). The Bible is specific about putting on Christ and becoming that which we are in Christ. Help the person see in which particular areas they need to grow: gratitude (key with sexual sin), humility, patience, joy and so on. Show them how being in Christ produces this in them.

8. **Direct** them to regulate their Christian life with regular times in the Word and prayer, leading them to pray specifically that God would help them take all desires and thoughts captive to Christ (2 Cor. 10:5). Also encourage wise inclusion

of others to whom they might be accountable in their fight for purity.

9. **Determine** to walk with them in the fellowship of the church, knowing that sin is stubborn and change can take time. And above all pray. Spiritual change is supernatural change. True, the person must work – that is non-negotiable. But as Paul says it is God who works in a person providing the ultimate transformation (Phil. 2:12-13). Therefore, it is to God that we appeal and in His sovereign grace we rest.

ACKNOWLEDGEMENTS

We wish to thank Willie Mackenzie for his partnership in this book. The team at CFP was characteristically excellent in their work on the project; we thank them for all their labors, with a special word of gratitude to Rosanna Burton.

Erik Wolgemuth provided terrific literary representation in this endeavor.

We thank the leadership of Midwestern Baptist Theological Seminary (Kansas City, Missouri) and Calvary Grace Church (Calgary, Alberta) for their support, and for slotting us roles that allow us to serve the church through writing. Dr Jason Allen is an exemplary seminary President, and Clint Humfrey is an exemplary pastor-theologian.

Our wives, Bethany Strachan and Amanda Peacock, persevered in a very busy writing season and offered encouragement throughout the process. We each send love to our wife.

This book is dedicated to two pastors who mentored us, taught us the sufficiency of Scripture for all of life, and gave us understanding about godly marriage and sexuality. What a gift these men were to us.

Above all, we thank the living God, and pray that He may continually help us and find us faithful on the last day.

About the Center for Biblical Sexuality

The Center for Biblical Sexuality (CBS) is a new initiative from Owen Strachan and Gavin Peacock. Primarily a website featuring resources on manhood, womanhood, biblical sexuality, the family, and more, the CBS offers biblical and theological clarity on the most pressing issues facing the global church in the areas of the body, personal identity, and sexuality. The mission statement of CBS: 'To strengthen the church and share Christ's love by answering pressing sexual questions with sound biblical doctrine.'

At the website, visitors will find long-form articles, multimedia content, links to helpful sites, and more. Please visit this new outlet at centerbiblicalsexuality.org.

**Also available by Owen Strachan
and Gavin Peacock...**

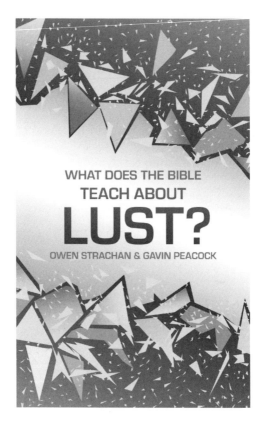

WHAT DOES THE BIBLE
TEACH ABOUT

LUST?

OWEN STRACHAN & GAVIN PEACOCK

What Does the Bible Teach About Lust?

A Short Book on Desire

Owen Strachan & Gavin Peacock

Lust is a problem. Our sexualised culture, promising freedom and pleasure, is creating a terrible cocktail of abuse, pain, despair, and suffering. The problem is not simply our actions, but our sinful desires. But there is hope. Christ is more powerful than any lustful desire, any temptation. He has defeated death and sin, and His way leads to true freedom.

978-1-5271-0476-1

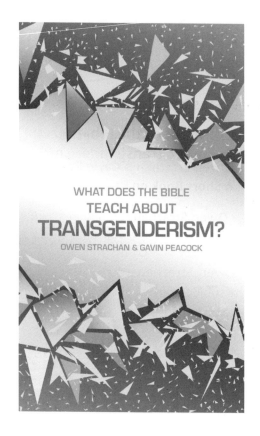

WHAT DOES THE BIBLE
TEACH ABOUT
TRANSGENDERISM?
OWEN STRACHAN & GAVIN PEACOCK

What Does the Bible Teach About Transgenderism?

A Short Book on Personal Identity

Owen Strachan & Gavin Peacock

Gender identity is a controversial and complex topic. Owen Strachan and Gavin Peacock dive into the subject with biblical clarity and the clear message of the gospel.

978-1-5271-0478-5

THE

GRAND

DESIGN

Male and Female He Made Them

OWEN STRACHAN

& GAVIN PEACOCK

The Grand Design

Male and Female He Made Them

Owen Strachan & Gavin Peacock

The world has gone gray-fuzzy, blurry, gender-neutral gray. In a secularist culture, many people today are confused about what it means to be a man or a woman. Even the church struggles to understand the meaning of manhood and womanhood. In *The Grand Design*, Owen Strachan and Gavin Peacock clear away the confusion and open up the Scriptures. They show that the gospel frees us to behold the unity and distinctiveness of the sexes. In Christ, we have a script for our lives. Doxology, we discover, is in the details.

What a great and timely book on the issue of the role and function of men and women. Concise and biblical, it deals with everything from marriage, manhood, womanhood, transgender and, of course, homosexuality; all issues facing Bible believing Christians in our day.

Mez McConnell
Pastor, Niddrie Community Church and Ministry
Director of 20Schemes

978-1-7819-1764-0

REENCHANTING
HUMANITY

A THEOLOGY OF MANKIND

OWEN STRACHAN

Reenchanting Humanity

A Theology of Mankind

Owen Strachan

Reenchanting Humanity is a work of systematic theology that focuses on the doctrine of humanity. Engaging the major anthropological questions of the age, like transgenderism, homosexuality, technology, and more, author Owen Strachan establishes a Christian anthropology rooted in Biblical truth, in stark contrast to the popular opinions of the modern age.

Not only is Strachan enjoyable to read, but I find that he helps me communicate traditional systematic assertions in arresting and memorable ways. I commend this volume to scholars, seminarians, and pastors as we seek to reflect faithfully on and teach clearly about all that God says in the Scriptures about man.

Ligon Duncan
Chancellor and CEO, Reformed Theological Seminary

978-1-5271-0502-7

Christian Focus Publications

Our mission statement —

STAYING FAITHFUL

In dependence upon God we seek to impact the world through literature faithful to His infallible Word, the Bible. Our aim is to ensure that the Lord Jesus Christ is presented as the only hope to obtain forgiveness of sin, live a useful life and look forward to heaven with Him.

Our books are published in four imprints:

CHRISTIAN FOCUS

Popular works including biographies, commentaries, basic doctrine and Christian living.

CHRISTIAN HERITAGE

Books representing some of the best material from the rich heritage of the church.

MENTOR

Books written at a level suitable for Bible College and seminary students, pastors, and other serious readers. The imprint includes commentaries, doctrinal studies, examination of current issues and church history.

CF4•K

Children's books for quality Bible teaching and for all age groups: Sunday school curriculum, puzzle and activity books; personal and family devotional titles, biographies and inspirational stories — because you are never too young to know Jesus!

Christian Focus Publications Ltd,
Geanies House, Fearn, Ross-shire,
IV20 1TW, Scotland, United Kingdom.

www.christianfocus.com
blog.christianfocus.com